W9-AHE-035

Lost and Found

Lost and Found

Helping Behaviorally Challenging Students
(and, While You're At It, All the Others)

ROSS W. GREENE, PhD

JB JOSSEY-BASS™

A Wiley Brand

Published by Jossey-Bass
A Wiley Brand
One Montgomery Street, Suite 1000, San Francisco, CA 94104-4594—www.josseybass.com

Jossey-Bass books and products are available through most bookstores. To contact Jossey-Bass directly call our Customer Care Department within the U.S. at 800-956-7739, out-side the U.S. at 317-572-3986, or fax 317-572-4002.

Wiley publishes in a variety of print and electronic formats and by print-on-demand. Some material included with standard print versions of this book may not be included in e-books or in print-on-demand. If this book refers to media such as a CD or DVD that is not included in the version you purchased, you may download this material at http://booksupport.wiley.com. For more information about Wiley products, visit www .wiley.com.

Library of Congress Cataloging-in-Publication Data has been Applied for and is on File with the Library of Congress.
ISBN: 978-1-118-89857-4 (hc)

Cover design by Wiley
Cover image: © Creatas/Thinkstock

Printed in the United States of America
FIRST EDITION
HB Printing   10 9 8

PREVIOUS BOOKS BY ROSS W. GREENE, PhD

The Explosive Child (1998)

Treating Explosive Kids (2005)

Lost at School (2008)

Raising Human Beings (2016)

CONTENTS

For my mom, Cynthia Greene . . . one of the most empathic, compassionate, resilient people I've known

ABOUT THE AUTHOR

Ross W. Greene, PhD, is the originator of the innovative, research-based approach now known as *Collaborative & Proactive Solutions* (CPS), as described in this book and his prior books *The Explosive Child* and *Lost at School*. Dr. Greene served on the teaching faculty at Harvard Medical School for over twenty years, and is currently adjunct associate professor in the Department of Psychology at Virginia Tech. He is also the founding director of the nonprofit Lives in the Balance (www.livesinthebalance.org), which provides a vast array of free, web-based resources on his model, and advocates on behalf of behaviorally challenging kids and their parents, teachers, and other caregivers. He is the author of numerous articles, chapters, and scientific papers on the effectiveness of the CPS model; the classification of and outcomes in youth with social, emotional, and behavioral challenges; and student-teacher compatibility. Dr. Greene lectures and consults to families, schools, inpatient psychiatry units, and residential and juvenile detention facilities throughout the world and lives with his family in Portland, Maine.

ACKNOWLEDGMENTS

I am indebted to my editor at Jossey-Bass, Margie McAneny, for her vision, guidance, perseverance, and boundless patience.

I am also grateful to the many teachers I've had over the years who helped me learn about the research, theories, and models of intervention that eventually gave rise to what is now known as Collaborative & Proactive Solutions, including social learning theory, family systems theory, transactional/reciprocal models of development, goodness-of-fit theory, neuropsychology, and developmental psychopathology. Those teachers include Dr. Elizabeth Altmaier (then at the University of Florida); Drs. Tom Ollendick and George Clum at the Department of Psychology at Virginia Tech; and Dr. Mary Ann McCabe and Lorraine Lougee, then at Children's National Medical Center in Washington, DC. And that's not even close to being an exhaustive list. My own two children—Talia and Jacob—have taught me plenty. Of course, my original teachers were my father, Irving (who is no longer with us), and my mother, Cynthia, to whom this book is dedicated.

But I am especially indebted to the thousands of classroom teachers I've had the good fortune to work with and learn from over the past twenty-five years. Despite working under very difficult circumstances, often thanklessly, you've taught me what a huge difference a teacher can make in a child's life, most especially those with social, emotional, and behavioral challenges who need someone to listen to them, nurture them, and help and care about them. You have my everlasting admiration.

INTRODUCTION

Welcome to *Lost and Found*. This book is intended as a follow-up to my earlier book *Lost at School*, which was first published in 2008. In that book, I described the manner in which the model of care I originated—now called *Collaborative & Proactive Solutions* (CPS)—is implemented in schools. The response to *Lost at School* has been heartening; the book has been translated into seventeen languages, and many thousands of schools across the world have relied on the book for guidance in transforming the ways in which students with social, emotional, and behavioral challenges are understood and treated.

So why write another book on the same topic? Because many of the very same educators and parents who found *Lost at School* to be helpful have told me they wanted more: more instruction on using the assessment instrumentation of the model (called the Assessment of Lagging Skills & Unsolved Problems [ALSUP]), more help in using and guiding others in the use of Plan B, and more information on organizing and sustaining the effort to transform discipline practices and implement the CPS model in a school. Those are the ingredients you'll find in the ensuing pages. Even if you haven't previously read *Lost at School*, all of the details of the CPS model are included in this book as well.

But the most exciting aspect of this book is that you'll be hearing from some of the amazing, courageous, visionary educators who have implemented the model in their schools and classrooms and with whom I've had the incredible privilege of collaborating. At the end of each chapter, there's a "Experience Is the Best Teacher" section that contains their wisdom. They're designated by their first names in each chapter; here are their full names:

Tom Ambrose, assistant superintendent in MSAD 52 in Maine (encompassing the towns of Greene, Leeds, and Turner)

Anonymous school principal, large urban school system

Kathy Bousquet, second-grade teacher, Central School, South Berwick, Maine

Alanna Craffey, second-grade teacher, Central School, South Berwick, Maine

Nina D'Aran, principal at Central School, South Berwick, Maine

Carol Davison, principal at Jessie Lee Elementary, Surrey, British Columbia, and former principal at Forsyth Road Elementary, Surrey

Ryan Gleason, assistant principal, Falmouth (Maine) Elementary School, and formerly at Durham (Maine) Community School

Katie Marshall, learning center teacher, Central School, South Berwick, Maine

Susan McCuaig, principal at T. E. Scott Elementary, Surrey, British Columbia, and former principal at Betty Huff Elementary, Surrey

Ryan Quinn, principal, Kennebunk Elementary School, Kennebunk, Maine

Vicki Stewart, director of communications at MSAD 35 in Maine and former principal at Central School

Brie Thomas, school counselor, Central School, South Berwick, Maine

They represent a small fraction of the many educators who have embraced the CPS model and have helped many thousands of vulnerable, at-risk children in the process.

The mission is no different than it was eight years ago: understand and help behaviorally challenging students in ways that are nonpunitive, nonadversarial, skill building, relationship enhancing, collaborative, proactive, and—most important—*helpful*. In too many schools, those ingredients are still missing. That's why rates of detention, suspension, and expulsion are still way too high, why schools in nineteen states in the United States still employ corporal punishment, why restraint and seclusion procedures are still employed hundreds of thousands of times in schools every year, and why there are still so many kids who feel disenfranchised, marginalized, disheartened, hopeless, and *lost*. To bring them back into the fold, we need to find our way to new lenses and new practices. And this needs to be a priority for every school.

The task is not made easier by the fact that classroom teachers have been given the very strong message that their job performance and security will be judged by how their students perform on high-stakes tests. While standards are a wonderful thing, the obsession with tests hasn't been good for classroom teachers or administrators or parents or behaviorally challenging students or any of the other students. But, as you'll be reading, many schools have accomplished the mission despite all the obstacles.

If you're brand new to the CPS model, many of your assumptions and practices may be called into question by what you read in the ensuing pages. That's OK; our knowledge of behaviorally challenging kids has expanded dramatically over the past forty to fifty years, and it turns out that a lot of what we were thinking about those kids—and doing to them—doesn't square up with what we now know about them. If you're already familiar with the CPS model, this book will take you further.

Finally, because this book is relevant to children of both genders . . . and because it is cumbersome to read *he or she, him or her,* and *his or her* throughout the book . . . and because I didn't want to write the book in one gender . . . entire chapters are written in alternating genders. I've drawn on a multitude of real kids and educators I've known and worked with in the dialogues in the book, but they are composites; any resemblance to people you may know is purely coincidental (but not necessarily surprising).

I'm looking forward to spending some time with you in the next nine chapters.

Ross Greene
Portland, Maine

Insanity is doing the same thing over and over again and expecting different results.

ALBERT EINSTEIN

Lost and Found

CHAPTER 1

THE WHO

Who are we talking about in this book? Naturally, we're talking about students whose difficulties meeting social, emotional, or behavioral expectations are expressed through severe behaviors. The ones who are screaming, swearing, hitting, biting, kicking, running out of the classroom, and worse. The ones who are flying frequently into the assistant principal's office. The ones who are on the receiving end of countless discipline referrals, detentions, suspensions, expulsions, physical and mechanical restraints, forced seclusions, and (yes, in many places, still in the year 2016), paddlings. That these interventions aren't working is made clear by the fact that they are being applied so frequently to the same students.

The ramifications of our lack of success with these students extend beyond the classroom. We find them in our statistics on dropping out, teenage pregnancy, substance abuse, and incarceration. These are also very expensive kids; placing a student in a program outside of the mainstream classroom is very costly. So the stakes are high, both in human and financial terms.

By the way, there are other students who are having difficulty meeting academic, social, and behavioral expectations, but whose behaviors are less extreme. They communicate that they're having difficulty by crying, sulking, pouting, withdrawing, becoming anxious, or sleeping through their classes. They may be sad that they have no friends, frustrated that they're having difficulty paying attention or sitting still, or hopeless over ongoing academic struggles. So we're talking about them, too.

Of course, when we don't effectively help behaviorally challenging students, their reasonably well-behaved classmates lose, too, and not merely in the ways that may be most obvious. Yes, there's lost learning. And there's the stress and anxiety of being around a kid who can be scary and seems out of control. But there's also the nagging sense that the adults aren't exactly sure what to do or how to make things better—because it's not getting better. And there's the uncomfortable feeling that the ways in which behaviorally challenging classmates are being treated are unnecessarily ostracizing and inhumane. So we're talking about the reasonably well behaved kids in this book, too.

We're also talking about classroom teachers. I don't come across many classroom teachers who look forward to dealing with their behaviorally challenging students on a daily basis (though there are exceptions). Those students—and their parents—are cited as a major contributing factor by many of the 50 percent of teachers who leave the profession within the first four years. And the emphasis on high-stakes testing has caused many classroom teachers to feel like test-prep robots, which, many tell me, has taken a lot of the humanity out of the work. Legislators and school boards often aren't focused on humanity; they're focused on test scores and new initiatives and budgets and reducing referrals into special education. The de-emphasis on social and emotional learning in many school systems has made it a lot harder to respond humanely in response to kids whose behavior is making everything else a lot more difficult. There's no *time* for humanity!

We're talking about parents, too. Parents of behaviorally challenging kids know a thing or two about feeling ostracized. They know they're blamed for their child's challenging behavior, despite the fact that they have other children who are well behaved. They don't want to be defensive, but feeling blamed doesn't make *that* any easier. They want to trust that their child is being well treated at school, but there are many signs to the contrary. Whatever the school is doing isn't working—their child is still on the receiving end of countless counseling sessions, detentions, suspensions and worse—but the parents feel powerless to do anything about it.

Of course, we're also talking about the parents of the reasonably well behaved kids. They may not know it, but they too have a stake in how things turn out with behaviorally challenging students. Their kids are showing up ready to learn, and the last thing they need is somebody else's kid screwing that up, making their child feel unsafe, and taking inordinate time and energy from the teacher. Not OK. Decisive action is needed, and pronto. Except that the pound of flesh and exclusion sometimes demanded by these parents isn't going to get the job done. When behaviorally challenging students aren't helped effectively, well-behaved kids and their parents suffer too.

If it's action that's called for, then we must also be talking about administrators. Most principals and assistant/vice principals aren't happy to have been placed in the role of building police officer. Yet the classroom teachers who are sending kids to the office also expect action, and are frequently quite clear about what the action should be: a powerful adult-imposed consequence—straight from the school's discipline handbook—that will finally get the message through and signal to the well-behaved students and their parents that the situation is being taken seriously and handled decisively. There's just that nagging awareness that the decisive and serious action *isn't actually working*. The kids who we've been sending to the office a lot are still being sent to the office a lot (if they haven't already dropped out of school). The line outside the principal's office is never-ending. Something's the matter with this picture.

Finally, we're also talking about school psychologists, counselors, social workers . . . the people who are officially on the hook for "fixing" students with social, emotional, and behavioral challenges. After all, it's often said, those students fall outside the expertise and responsibility of the general education classroom teacher. The problem, of course, is that the building's school mental health designee is overwhelmed, too. He or she may be covering several different schools, the kids who need help just keep on coming, and the testing load is intense. Plus, shouldn't the people who have been sending the kid to the office be involved in the process of helping these kids instead of handing the kid off like a hot potato to someone else?

Apparently, we're talking about everybody. And that's good, because when we help behaviorally challenging students more effectively, we're helping everybody else too. And it's going to take everybody to turn things around.

So now, the question: Are the ways in which we're dealing with behaviorally challenging kids at school actually helping? And another: Do the traditional disciplinary strategies even make sense anymore, given what we now know about behaviorally challenging kids? If not, then we're helping no one.

We've lost our way. We need to find a different way.

That starts with taking a look at what we've been thinking about behaviorally challenging kids. The lenses through which we're viewing these kids will have a major influence on the stance we take toward them and the strategies we employ in our efforts to help. What we're thinking and seeing and doing should be a reflection of the mountain of research on behaviorally challenging kids that has accumulated over the past forty to fifty years.

Here's what we've *been* thinking: behaviorally challenging kids are attention seeking, manipulative, unmotivated, coercive, and limit testing. And the parents of those kids are passive, permissive, inconsistent, noncontingent disciplinarians.

> *Challenging kids are challenging because they're lacking the skills to not be challenging.*

The problem, of course, is that those beliefs are not a reflection of what the research tells us about behaviorally challenging kids. What we now know can be summarized in one sentence: *challenging kids are challenging because they're lacking the skills to not be challenging.* In other words, challenging behavior is reflective of a *developmental delay.* We'll be thinking more about that notion in subsequent chapters. But, for now, it's important to note that the emphasis is on lagging *skills,* not lagging *motivation.* That's an important distinction because, generally speaking, strategies aimed at improving motivation do not improve lagging skills. And the discipline programs in most schools are still oriented toward improving motivation.

Two ingredients are required for a student to behave adaptively: *motivation* and *skills.* For a very long time, school discipline programs have been focused on the *motivation* part, when the research tells us that we should instead have been focused on the *skills* part—just as we would with any other developmental delay.

As you may already know, the Collaborative & Proactive Solutions (CPS) model described in this book operates on a very important key theme:

KIDS DO WELL IF THEY CAN

This is the belief that if the kid *could* do well, he *would* do well, and that if he's not doing well, he must be lacking the skills to do well. One of the most important things a potential helper can do for a behaviorally challenging student is to finally, at long last, figure out what skills the child is lacking. Those lagging skills are making it difficult for the student to meet certain academic and behavioral expectations.

> The other important thing a potential helper can do for a behaviorally challenging student is to identify the *expectations* the student is having difficulty meeting. In the CPS model, those unmet expectations are referred to as *unsolved problems.*

Here's another key theme, and it's related to the first:

DOING WELL IS PREFERABLE

This is the belief that human beings—behaviorally challenging kids included—have a strong preference for doing well (as opposed to doing poorly). This belief is at odds with the commonly held belief that a student's challenging behavior is *working* for him.

How would challenging behavior be working? According to conventional notions about the *function* of behavior, challenging behavior helps a student *get* something (for example, attention) and helps him *escape* and *avoid* tasks that are tedious, challenging, uncomfortable, or scary. If that's what we're thinking and seeing, the interventions that make perfect sense are those aimed at proving to the student that his challenging behavior isn't going to work, and trying to elicit and encourage replacement behaviors that adults believe will work better. The first goal is typically accomplished through use of punishment, the second through use of reward.

But *all* of us get, escape, and avoid. So the question isn't whether the student is getting, escaping, and avoiding, but rather *why the student is going about getting, escaping, and avoiding in such a maladaptive manner.* And now you have the answer, thanks to the mountain of research: *because he's lacking the skills to get, escape, and avoid in a more adaptive fashion.* If we don't yet know what skills a student is lacking, and we don't yet know what expectations a student is having difficulty meeting, then we don't yet know how to help the student.

What skills does the research tell us behaviorally challenging kids are lacking? For the time being, we're going to sacrifice precision for simplicity: *flexibility/adaptability*, *frustration tolerance*, and *problem solving*. Challenging episodes typically occur when these skills are being demanded. Along these lines, here's another crucial true fact: *Challenging kids aren't always challenging; they're only sometimes challenging*. When are they challenging? *When the demands and expectations being placed on them outstrip the skills they have to respond adaptively.* Just like the rest of us.

> *Adult-imposed consequences don't teach kids the skills they lack or solve the problems that set the stage for their challenging behavior.*

When we treat behaviorally challenging kids as if they have a developmental delay and apply the same compassion and pretty much the same approach we would use with any other learning disability, they do a lot better. When we continue treating them as if they're unmotivated, manipulative, attention seeking, and limit testing and continue relying heavily on adult-imposed consequences, they often don't do better. Again, that's because adult-imposed consequences don't teach kids the skills they lack or solve the problems that set the stage for their challenging behavior.

Let's think briefly about the word *helper*, because that's the most important role caregivers can play in the life of a behaviorally challenging student. Of course, educators are in one of the helping professions; so are parents, mental health professionals, coaches, medical doctors, and so forth. There are two criteria for being an effective helper:

1. **Helpers help.** In other words, helpers abide by the Hippocratic Oath, which goes something like this: *don't make it worse*.

2. *Helpers have thick skin.* In other words, helpers don't take
    things personally. While helpers are entitled to their feelings,
    helpers bend over backward to ensure that those feelings do
    not interfere with helping.

In many schools, the interventions that are still being applied
to behaviorally challenging kids are making things worse. And in
many schools, helpers' subjective reactions and inaccurate beliefs
about the difficulties of these students is interfering with helping.

If the lenses and interventions that are being applied to behaviorally challenging students in a particular building aren't
helping, then we will continue to lose those students. And, as
you've already read, when those students lose, we all lose. Changing course—finding a different way—requires that the helpers
recognize that. And then start the hard work of doing things
differently.

So now let's get back to where we started at the beginning of
this chapter. Who are we talking about in this book?

Everyone.

CHAPTER 2

THE MESS

It's a jungle out there for behaviorally challenging kids. Many of the developments and initiatives that have come down the pike in the last twenty to thirty years have made it much harder for their teachers and other school staff to fulfill the role of helper. Zero-tolerance policies have made things worse. The research tells us it's so. Those policies turned potential helpers into disciplinary robots, and caused them to respond to behavioral challenges with algorithms rather than rational thought, as adversaries rather than as partners, with consequences rather than collaboration. Although some school systems have abandoned those policies, they still resonate in the mind-sets of many educators. Perhaps this explains why, in the United States alone, we still expel over one hundred thousand students from public school annually, suspend more than three million times a year (that's probably an underestimate), dole out countless dozens of millions of detentions and discipline referrals every year, use restraint and seclusion procedures 270,000 times a year, and—in nineteen states—still apply corporal punishment hundreds of thousands of times a year (disproportionately to children of color). One of the most important doctrines governing interventions for students who receive special education in US public schools is the principle of the *least restrictive environment.* A similar doctrine—the *least toxic response*—should be applied to interventions for behaviorally challenging students. Detention, suspension, expulsion, paddling, and restraint and seclusion fall into the most toxic response category.

> *The* least toxic response . . . *should be applied to interventions for behaviorally challenging students. Detention, suspension, expulsion, paddling, and restraint and seclusion fall into the most toxic response category.*

What the school-to-prison-pipeline research tells us is that the students who are most likely to access the school discipline program—the frequent flyers, as they're known—are the ones who benefit from it the least. Who, then, is benefiting from the school discipline program? Clearly not the behaviorally challenging students. But not the well-behaved students either. The well-behaved students aren't behaving themselves because of the school discipline program. They're behaving themselves because they *can.*

Doesn't a suspension at least give the teachers and the well-behaved students a break from behaviorally challenging students? Sure, for about three days. Then she's back, and with all of the same problems that set in motion the challenging behaviors that prompted the suspension in the first place. Along with, eventually, an attitude, which is what most of us would have if caregivers who were supposed to be helping continued to apply interventions that weren't helping and that, in fact, had the primary effect of pushing us away.

High-stakes testing hasn't helped. It has caused many educators to feel like test-prep robots. When we tell teachers that their job performance and security will be judged by how their students do well on mandated tests, we increase the likelihood that teachers will devote most of their energy to helping students do well on mandated tests. Anything that interferes with that mission must be dealt with immediately and severely. And where does this leave the students who are disrupting the class, interfering with the learning of their classmates, and consuming an inordinate amount of time? It leaves them being dealt with immediately and severely, which is both ineffective and unhelpful. And that, of course, just takes more time.

By the way, classroom teachers aren't the only ones stressed out by high-stakes testing and other indices of skill, achievement, and talent; a lot of students are stressed out by it too. The competition and pressure to obtain high test scores and get admitted into premium colleges are, in many communities, ridiculously intense.

But the societal shifts that have worked to the disadvantage of kids over the past forty or fifty years aren't limited to schools. Things are more stressful at home, too. It now takes two incomes to maintain the lifestyle that one income previously supported. The rate of kids living in single-parent homes has doubled in the last fifty years. So a lot of kids don't have the level of contact and interaction with their parents that they might have had three or four decades ago.

The budget cuts haven't helped. Class sizes in many school systems are larger—in some places, much larger—and in many places, extra support for kids with special needs has been cut. Those cuts have disproportionately affected schools in low-income neighborhoods.

> *Using diagnoses as the gatekeeper for services, placement, and funding simply guarantees that about 50 percent of the kids who we already know need our help won't get it.*

The emphasis on psychiatric diagnoses as the gatekeeper for services, placement, and funding hasn't helped at all. Many kids with social, emotional, and behavioral challenges badly need help but don't meet diagnostic criteria for any particular psychiatric disorder. Indeed, using diagnoses as the gatekeeper simply guarantees that about 50 percent of the kids who we already know need our help won't get it. And those diagnoses—which are just long lists of maladaptive behaviors thought to cluster together—cause us to focus on *behaviors* rather than on the lagging skills and unsolved problems that are contributing to those behaviors.

The special education referral process often doesn't help. It has just dramatically increased the testing loads of school psychologists. For many classroom teachers concerned about a student, a psycho-educational evaluation often feels like the only option for obtaining additional information about the student's difficulties. But the evaluation process can take a long time, and is often geared toward determining only whether a student qualifies for special services, so the teachers are often disappointed in and underwhelmed by the information they've been waiting for.

The countless initiatives aimed at improving students' academic and social/emotional outcomes—many imposed by legislators, few of whom have spent any time in a school classroom—haven't helped. Well, maybe some of them have moved the ball forward, but there are just too many of them. Many teachers and administrators will whisper that their superiors are enamored with initiatives because it makes them look as though they're accomplishing something. But all those initiatives aren't necessarily good for the kids. And they're not good for the people who are on the hook for implementing them. And unless they're legislatively mandated, the initiatives tend to die after a quick burst of energy or enthusiasm, or when the funding runs out, or when an administration changes.

Many of the popular behavior initiatives that have come down the pike haven't helped, not enough anyway. They haven't been transformative enough to fundamentally alter the lenses through which we view behaviorally challenging students and the interventions that are applied to them. And the anti-bullying programs haven't necessarily reduced bullying. In many places, they've simply provided justification for bullying the bullies.

> *Classroom teachers have historically been among the most important agents of socialization for our children. But when we force teachers to become disciplinary and test-prep robots, we take the humanity out of the job.*

Classroom teachers have historically been among the most important agents of socialization for our children. But when we force teachers to become disciplinary and test-prep robots, we take the humanity out of the job. Given the trends I've described here, we need to help teachers be humane and compassionate now more than ever. We need them to foster the skills in their students that bring out the more positive side of human nature: empathy, appreciating how one's behavior is affecting others, taking another's perspective, honesty, resolving disagreements in ways that do not involve conflict. We need schools to be safe havens for learning and social development. Not just for the behaviorally challenging kids. For all kids.

No wonder schools are feeling less safe these days. As of this writing, there have been at least seventy-nine shootings in elementary, middle, junior, and high schools since Newtown. That's not a misprint. That's a signal.

There are many factors that stack the odds against educators that make it more difficult for them to help. Yet, helping teachers be helpers is imperative. There's a lot at stake.

EXPERIENCE IS THE BEST TEACHER

❝ I remember my first few years as assistant principal before implementing CPS in our school. Students were lined up outside my office for various behavioral issues on a frequent basis. Since I thought of myself as the 'fix-it' person, my goal was to resolve the situation as quickly as possible. I wanted to support the teacher and help the student become more successful, but the same students, often sent from the same teachers, seemed to return over and over again. I always felt that there had to be a better way to do this.❞❞

—RYAN, ASSISTANT PRINCIPAL

❝❝Sometimes it's hard for teachers to let go of more traditional mind-sets or practices. Because they believe that their job is to get kids ready for the next grade. It's just their mind-set that everybody should be pushed as hard as they can and everyone should get the same thing because that's what's fair.❞❞

—NINA, PRINCIPAL

❝❝My first job right out of high school was at a day care, working with five-year-olds. I was taught that if a kid is hitting another child, then you take her over to the corner and you leave her there for three minutes. And even though intuitively I thought, 'This is not teaching her anything,' I felt like I had to do my job. That's what I was taught to do. *The behavior's not going to happen again because I taught them a lesson, I hoped; I've shown the student that I'm in control and I'm the boss.* When I started teaching in the classroom, it was the same thing. I worried I'd get in trouble if I didn't enforce the school rules.❞❞

—BRIE, SCHOOL COUNSELOR

❝❝I always think about kids getting suspended. How does that solve the problem? That just pushes them away.❞❞

—KATIE, LEARNING CENTER TEACHER

❝❝It's trying to extinguish the behavior, but it's not solving the problem.❞❞

—VICKI, DIRECTOR OF COMMUNICATIONS

❝❝Suspending kids doesn't help build a relationship with them; it says, 'We don't want you here.'❞❞

—CAROL, PRINCIPAL

❝It says we're giving up on you. You can't do it. Get out. You're not good enough. I mean, what's the unspoken message that we give children when we do that? I'm not saying that there aren't instances that I feel would warrant taking a child out of the environment, but there's a serious level of responsibility on the part of adults for the message that we're sending kids.❞

—TOM, ASSISTANT SUPERINTENDENT

❝I've seen kids removed from riding the school bus as a way to teach them how we expect them to conduct themselves on the school bus. But it doesn't make any sense to remove a kid from the school bus to teach her how to conduct herself on the school bus. How is that going to change anything about the factors that are making it difficult for the student to meet our expectations on the school bus?❞

—CAROL, PRINCIPAL

❝I find that most of the teachers I work with are very in tune with kids' individual needs, and they're more than happy to try something to help our students feel more successful and solve some of those problems that are getting in their way.❞

—NINA, PRINCIPAL

❝My population is 95 percent African American and Hispanic, 80 to 85 percent male, and between 25 and 50 percent special education. The fact that we have criminalized discipline in our school system—especially with students who have certain profiles—helps explain why we lose these students. School becomes a puzzle they cannot solve. There is huge drop in suspensions after the tenth grade only because many of my students never get past their sophomore year. They just stop accruing credit. Suspension is a political hot potato, so schools are trying to keep those numbers down. The students who were being suspended repeatedly are still struggling to meet expectations. Schools are just becoming much better at massaging the data.❞

—ANONYMOUS SCHOOL PRINCIPAL

CHAPTER 3

THE SHIFT

Clearly, some dramatic changes are needed to better help students with social, emotional, and behavioral challenges. The lenses and practices provided by the CPS model are encompassed by six key themes. In chapter 1, you were introduced to two of them.

KEY THEME 1: KIDS DO WELL IF THEY CAN

This contrasts with the traditional mentality, "Kids do well if they want to," and makes it clear that motivational strategies—adult-imposed consequences—will not be the focal point of intervention. The *Kids do well if they can* mentality settles the *can't* versus *won't* debate in favor of *can't*. Even if the student *can* meet a given expectation *sometimes*, you're on the hook for figuring out what's getting in the way of his meeting the expectation *consistently*.

> ## KEY THEME 2: DOING WELL IS PREFERABLE
>
> *Doing well is preferable* makes it clear that we'll be moving well beyond the traditional belief that the primary function of challenging behavior is getting, escaping, and avoiding. The true function of challenging behavior is that it *communicates* that a student is lacking the skills to handle certain demands and expectations. In other words, the behavior is simply the signal, the fever. This alternative definition of function helps us move beyond behavior and diagnoses, and focus on the factors that are truly getting in the way for the student—namely, the skills he's lacking and the expectations he's having difficulty reliably meeting (again in the CPS model, those unmet expectations are referred to as unsolved problems).

Here are the remaining themes:

> ## KEY THEME 3: THE IMPORTANT STUFF IS UPSTREAM
>
> Whereas many caregivers have been trained to focus on kids' *challenging behavior*—and *modifying* it—that's not what you're focused on and doing in the CPS model. You're instead focused on the *problems* that are giving rise to those behaviors and *solving them.* In other words, behavior is what's going on *downstream*; the problems that are causing those behaviors are awaiting discovery and resolution *upstream*. In the CPS model, you're focused almost exclusively on what's going on upstream.

The reality is that a student's challenging behavior isn't especially informative, especially as it relates to *why* the student is exhibiting that behavior. As the field of developmental psychopathology tells us, the same challenging behavior can be caused by a wide variety of different risk factors (a concept known as equifinality), and the same risk factor can set in motion a wide range of different challenging behaviors (a concept known as multifinality). Yet, in school meetings—the ones in which we're discussing behaviorally challenging students—much time is devoted to detailed descriptions of a student's challenging *behavior* and caregivers' *explanations* for that behavior. *If challenging behavior is all we focus on in our discussions and meetings, then we will be led only to interventions that focus on modifying that behavior. And if we rely only on caregivers' theories and explanations for the cause of that behavior, then we'll never gather the information that truly helps us understand what's making it hard for the student to meet certain expectations.*

> *One of the reasons the problems of behaviorally challenging students often remain unsolved is that we haven't been focused on identifying those problems; we've instead been focused on the by-products of those problems (the behaviors).*

One of the reasons the problems of behaviorally challenging students often remain unsolved is that we haven't been focused on identifying those problems; we've instead been focused on the by-products of those problems (the behaviors). And one thing is fairly certain: if you're focused on the behaviors, you won't know what problems you're trying to solve . . . and they won't get solved.

Of course, much meeting time is also devoted to discussing the psychiatric diagnoses that summarize a student's challenging behaviors, especially if those challenging behaviors cluster together into one of the categories that can be found in the most current diagnostic manual. But, as you've read, diagnoses aren't especially informative either, especially when it comes to the two most important questions that need to be answered for us to better help behaviorally challenging students: *why* (as in, *Why* is this student exhibiting challenging behavior?) and *when* (as in, *When* is this student exhibiting challenging behavior?). Fortunately, as you've read, we know the answer to both questions. Why are challenging kids challenging? Because they're lacking skills. When are challenging kids challenging? When the expectations being placed on them exceed their skills. Those questions—why and when—must be answered for each behaviorally challenging student we're trying to help.

Indeed, while the categorical approach to summarizing mal-adaptive behaviors can be useful in some ways, I often find that it often does more harm than good. That being the case, it's often far more productive to move away from the obsession with categories and view challenging behavior as occurring on a spectrum. At the easy end of the spectrum are relatively mild behaviors like crying, sulking, pouting, whining, and withdrawing. More severe behaviors would include screaming, swearing, spitting, hitting, kicking, destroying property, lying, and truancy. And at the extreme end of the spectrum are such behaviors as self-induced vomiting, cutting, substance abuse, stabbing, and shooting. But all of these behaviors occur under the same conditions: *when the demands being placed on a kid exceed the kid's capacity to respond adaptively.* Why do some kids more easily and adaptively handle the myriad social, academic, and behavioral demands being placed on them at school? You already know the answer to that question, too: because they can. They have the skills to do it.

Fifty years ago, a psychiatrist named Thomas Szasz understood that mental health diagnoses were very restrictive in helping us understand people with social, emotional, and behavioral challenges. He advocated for reconceptualizing these challenges as "problems in living." He hit the nail right on the head.

This shift in focus has significant implications for assessment. Most of the assessment tools employed in schools—behavior observations, behavior checklists, functional behavior assessments (FBAs)—are focused on a student's *behaviors*. In the CPS model, assessment focuses on identifying the lagging skills and unsolved problems that are making it difficult for the student to meet our behavioral expectations.

KEY THEME 4: THE PROBLEM SOLVING IS COLLABORATIVE, NOT UNILATERAL

If we're going to be in the problem-solving business, we'd better think about what kind of problem solving we want to be doing. Caregivers, including those in education, tend to favor problem solving of the *uni-lateral* variety. This is where the adult determines the solution and imposes it on the kid. But that's not what you're doing in the CPS model. In this model, the problem solving is of the *collaborative* variety.

> *Solving problems is something you're doing with the student, not to him.*

The CPS model operates on a very important assumption: if you want to solve a problem with a kid—any kid, but especially the behaviorally challenging variety—you're a lot better off if you have a *partner*. . . a teammate. Who's your teammate? The student, your new problem-solving partner. In other words, solving problems is something you're doing *with* the student, not *to* him. Solving the problems that are causing challenging behavior doesn't need to be adversarial. Kids—and everyone else—are a whole lot more receptive to participating in solving the problems that are affecting their lives when you're solving problems *with* them rather than doing something *to* them.

KEY THEME 5: THE PROBLEM SOLVING IS PROACTIVE, NOT REACTIVE

If we want to solve problems collaboratively, we should also consider our timing. A great deal of the intervention that takes place with behaviorally challenging kids in schools occurs in the heat of the moment, emergently, reactively. But, as it relates to solving problems collaboratively, that's actually terrible (and unnecessary) timing. In the CPS model, 99 percent of intervention takes place proactively.

This theme, of course, often prompts a very important question: How can we solve problems proactively when we never know when the kid is going to exhibit challenging behavior . . . when he's so unpredictable? The answer: we do know when he's going to exhibit challenging behavior, and he's not unpredictable . . . if we put the hard work into figuring it out on the front end. Figuring it out involves answering those two questions (why and when) and—as you shall see in the next chapter—one single-sided sheet of paper.

KEY THEME 6: UNDERSTANDING IS THE MOST IMPORTANT PART OF HELPING

As you've read, a large body of research has accumulated over the last forty to fifty years to help us better understand why challenging kids are challenging. For the rest of the book, you'll be reading about how this dramatic improvement in our understanding of behaviorally challenging kids should change our intervention practices. For now, let's think about how it changes our lenses, because what you see is what you get.

First, there's a huge difference between viewing a child's behavioral challenges as a sign of lacking motivation versus understanding that he's lacking skills. Once this conceptual hurdle has been cleared, caregivers become more compassionate, their explanations become more accurate, and their interventions become more effective. And there are many things they stop saying:

"He just wants attention."
We all want attention, so this explanation isn't very useful for helping us understand why a kid is seeking attention in a maladaptive manner. If a kid is seeking attention in a maladaptive way, that simply suggests that he lacks the skills to seek atten-

tion in an adaptive way. Again, kids do well if they can, and doing well is preferable.

"He just wants his own way."

We all want our own way, too, so this statement doesn't help us understand why this student is trying to get his own way in ways that are so maladaptive. Adaptively getting one's own way requires skills often found lacking in challenging kids. And it takes two to tango: in every power struggle between a child and an adult, there's an adult who wants his or her own way, too.

"He's manipulating us."

This is a very popular, and misguided, characterization of kids with behavioral challenges. Competent manipulation requires various skills—forethought, planning, impulse control, and organization, among others—typically found lacking in behaviorally challenging kids. In other words, the kids who are most often described as being manipulative are those least capable of doing it well.

"He's not motivated."

This is something we should never say about any kid. Once we figure out what's really getting in the way for kids being referred to as unmotivated, we find that "unmotivated" didn't even come close to capturing the factors making it difficult for the child to meet our expectations. Moreover, why would any kid not want to do well? Why would he choose not to do well if he has the skills to do well? *Skills* are the engine pulling the train; motivation is the caboose.

"He's making bad choices."

He's probably lacking the skills needed for consistently making good choices.

> *Skills are the engine pulling the train; motivation is the caboose.*

HELPING

What are the two most important roles a helper can play in the life of a behaviorally challenging student?

1. **Figure out what skills the student is lacking and the expectations he's having difficulty meeting**. As you've read, we'll be referring to those unmet expectations as *unsolved problems.*
2. **Start solving those problems;** but do it in a way—**collaboratively and proactively**—that engages the child in solving the problems that affect his life, creates a problem-solving partnership, and simultaneously teaches the child the skills he's lacking.

Those are two things adult-imposed consequences won't accomplish. A sticker chart won't, nor will depriving a child of recess. Sending the child to the office won't, nor would a detention or suspension. And, let there be no doubt, paddling the child won't help caregivers accomplish those two things.

When we identify the skills a student is lacking and the expectations he is having difficulty meeting, the student's challenging episodes become highly predictable. Intervention becomes proactive.

Q & A

Question: But we've always used incentive programs in my building. Should we stop?

Answer: Most schools have been using incentive programs for a very long time. But when I ask school staff why they're still using incentive-based programs, the most common response they give—while simultaneously telling me that those programs aren't working for many of the kids they're trying to help—is "because it's the way we've always done it." Of course, if the way we've always done it isn't working for the kids we've always done it to, we probably ought to stop doing it and think of something better to do.

Question: Does this mean that consequences should no longer be applied to challenging behavior?

Answer: It's important to distinguish between the two types of consequences: *natural* and *adult-imposed.* Natural consequences—being liked or disliked, being included or excluded, feeling happy or ashamed by one's behavior, doing well or poorly on an exam—are very powerful and persuasive. They're also inevitable. Of course, natural consequences don't solve the problems that are causing a kid's challenging behavior. So when the challenging behavior persists, or worsens, adults typically add even more consequences, those of the adult-imposed, "logical," "unnatural," or "artificial" variety. These include punishments, such as staying in from recess, detention, suspension, and paddling; and rewards, such as stickers, happy faces, points, and special privileges. Adult-imposed consequences are also very powerful and persuasive. But adult-imposed consequences don't solve the problems that are causing a kid's challenging behavior either. So in instances where the very powerful and persuasive *natural* consequences don't get the job done—and now we're talking about most behaviorally challenging kids—it's not exactly clear why adding *more* consequences would accomplish the mission. Moreover, adult-imposed consequences cause a child to look outside of himself rather than inside of himself for guidance on how to behave. We want kids looking inside, not outside, for that guidance. The students who are on the receiving end of endless natural and adult-imposed consequences clearly need something else from us.

Question: Does the alternative definition of *function* mean that we should stop doing functional behavior assessments (FBAs)?

Answer: No, FBAs are a wonderful thing, but only when we stop coming to the automatic belief that a student's behavior is *working*, and that the behavior is effective at helping the student *get, escape,* and *avoid.* FBAs are a lot more meaningful and informative when we view challenging behavior as the means by which the student is communicating that he's lacking the skills to meet certain demands and expectations, and then document which skills the student is lacking and which expectations the student is having difficulty meeting. I've had way too many classroom teachers tell me that there's really no point in reading a student's FBA because all FBAs say the exact same thing. If all FBAs say the exact same thing, then those are perfunctory, boilerplate FBAs, not useful, informative, meaningful FBAs.

> *Adult-imposed consequences cause a child to look outside of himself rather than inside of himself for guidance on how to behave. We want kids looking inside, not outside, for that guidance.*

Question: So we can't just do nothing in response to challenging behavior! Consequences at least help us feel like we're doing something. What should we do instead?

Answer: Not relying on adult-imposed consequences doesn't mean you're doing nothing. It means you've come to recognize the limitations of that form of intervention. There's no reason to continue doing something if that something isn't getting the job done. As for what you'll be doing instead, that's what the rest of the book is about.

Question: What do we say to the well-behaved kids when they observe that they're behaviorally challenging classmates are being treated differently or aren't receiving the consequences that are usually applied to misbehavior?

Answer: We point out the realities. The consequences weren't working very well anyway. You're working hard on the problem and intend to keep everyone safe. Fair doesn't mean equal. In every classroom, different kids are being treated differently, according to their needs, and that approach benefits everyone, including the well-behaved students. Behavioral differences should be handled no differently than academic differences.

EXPERIENCE IS THE BEST TEACHER

❝❝I came to CPS because I hit that wall of futility and realized that no matter how many consequences I kept giving to these kids, nothing was going to change. I needed to change, and I needed to change how I was viewing them and dealing with them. It seems like we're often in a mind-set of, 'This kid is broken. This kid needs fixing. He needs a doctor.' I had to turn the mirror around and ask, 'Let's look at what *we're* doing, too.'❞❞

—NINA, PRINCIPAL

❝❝We began using CPS in our building because we were having difficulties helping a particular student. We had really tried to come up with different things that would help him and work with him, but we didn't have the language, we didn't know about CPS, and we were just coming from the good part of our hearts of wanting to help a child who we knew wanted to do well but was really having a hard time. This is a kid who was doing things that were physically dangerous to himself, like banging his head on the floor. His mom would have to drag him out of the car to bring him to school. We were trying really hard to figure out what was going on with him, but before we learned about CPS, we never asked the most important person: him.❞❞

—KATHY, TEACHER

❝❝With that student, we were focused on behaviors, not the problems that were causing the behaviors. It would be something as simple as writing, and he'd rip up his paper. So instead of trying to figure out what was getting in his way on a particular writing assignment, we'd ask him why he was ripping up his paper. Or we'd tell him that we don't tolerate that kind of behavior at school. Or I would have told him what he should be doing instead. Or we'd go for a walk; we'd distract him. But we weren't finding out what his concerns were. Once we started talking about problems instead of behaviors . . . once we built a relationship with him . . . he started to feel a lot more comfortable.❞❞

—KATIE, LEARNING CENTER TEACHER

❝❝Working in a building where behavioral incentives have been a traditional part of the culture, I often have staff members question the philosophy of extrinsic versus intrinsic motivation. Teachers would ask, 'Shouldn't students want to do well for the sake of doing well, not just to earn something?' The CPS model answers that question with a resounding yes with the fundamental beliefs that *kids do well if they can,* not *kids do well if they want to.* When you start with that shift in thinking, it leads you in different and more productive directions to help and support students in finding success.❜❜

—Ryan, ASSISTANT PRINCIPAL

❛❛I was skeptical about CPS. I have a very intense behavioral background. I was steeped in the whole routine of applying consequences for undesirable behavior and rewarding positive behavior. So CPS was like learning a whole new language for me. It was like discovering that the sky was purple; I didn't realize that there was another world out there. At first, I really struggled. I wanted to be able to embrace it, but it just didn't make sense. Eventually I found it productive to question my old beliefs and practices. I think having a disabled child myself, and having him go through school, helped to change my perspective. I forbade his school from giving him time-outs; I didn't want him to be punished for things related to his neurologically based condition— things that stickers and punishment weren't going to change. So I think having my son helped me see other behaviorally challenging kids through different lenses. And then, when I understood CPS, it was like, 'Wow.' But one of the biggest hurdles is that even today, teachers are being trained to use carrots and sticks as their primary classroom management tools.❜❜

—Anonymous, EDUCATIONAL TECHNICIAN

❛❛My daughter's getting her master's in special education, and she's never heard of CPS.❜❜

—Alanna, TEACHER

❛❛You can't fault teachers for wanting to give kids more and more consequences. As a school leader, you have to listen to why teachers feel they need those consequences. With one teacher, she was feeling that her class was spinning out of control. And she was sort of feeling like, 'If I don't get this child under control now, I'll lose control of the whole group, and I won't get anything taught this year.'❜❜

—Nina, PRINCIPAL

❛❛I had one student who, when he was out of control, would rip things off the wall. And there was a kindergarten teacher who said to me, 'He needs to put all that stuff back on the wall the way it was.' And I said, 'Well, he could, but that's not going to solve the problems that are causing him to rip things off the wall.' And so the teacher started thinking about it, and she got it.**" "**

—ANONYMOUS, EDUCATIONAL TECHNICIAN

" "There's no quick fix. And I think sometimes people use punishment thinking they can bring a bad situation under control right away, but it doesn't work that way. I had a kid in the office the other day who was having trouble getting his work done in class, and he just lay on the rug in the office and wouldn't say anything. And I said, 'Well, I can see that you're having a hard time.' So I let him lay there for a while. And I said, 'Maybe we could have lunch today and problem-solve. Thumbs up if you can do that.' And he put his thumb up. And then, a couple minutes later, he was able to talk. If all I did was think about what punishment he should get, he never would have talked, and the problem never would have been solved.**" "**

—NINA, PRINCIPAL

" "The behavioral approach is often applied in ways that are so adversarial. It's like, 'I'm in control. And you're going to do it my way.' There are so many power plays and power struggles that I see teachers get into with their students.**" "**

—ANONYMOUS, EDUCATIONAL TECHNICIAN

" "These kids who are receiving endless consequences . . . they often feel like the world is out to get them. So they project that they don't care. If that's the case, then the place to start is by building a relationship, and that's what may eventually restore things. But the student probably didn't get to the point of not caring overnight, so I wouldn't expect that we're going to solve all of his problems overnight either. I mean, you've got to work with him for a while.**" "**

—TOM, ASSISTANT SUPERINTENDENT

" "That's one of the biggest things that came out of implementing CPS in my school: many classroom teachers had no idea that they could have this powerful impact with kids through the relationships they were building with them and the problem-solving discussions they were having with them.**" "**

—SUSAN, PRINCIPAL

❝ When I first learned that challenging behaviors were due to lagging skills, it was like a lightbulb went on. It's what I'd been thinking; I just never really had words for it. ❞

—KATIE, LEARNING CENTER TEACHER

❝ I think the belief that *kids do well if they can* cultivates in kids the recognition that doing the right thing is OK in its own right . . . not just because they're being told to do something or not to do it, or because they're being given a reward for doing it. ❞

—TOM, ASSISTANT SUPERINTENDENT

❝ We're all just human beings, and we all exhibit challenging behaviors from time to time. We need different lenses for understanding why the student is having difficulty meeting an expectation, because I think that, way too often, we're just trying to control the situation instead of looking deeper. ❞

—CAROL, PRINCIPAL

❝ Everybody knows what the kid's challenging behaviors are—you can figure that out in two seconds—but you have to go deeper. ❞

—NINA, PRINCIPAL

❝ It drives me crazy when I hear people say that kids can make better choices, because, nine times out of ten, it wasn't a choice; it was a reaction, it was an impulse, it was the best option the child had at that moment. It wasn't really, 'Hmm, should I punch that kid in the face because he just dissed my mom, or should I talk about it?' If the kid punches, that tells us that the demands of the situation outstripped his skills in that moment. So it seems to me that we need to take a step back and have that more objective lens, like what are these really specific demands that I'm putting on the students, and why are they not able to meet those demands? ❞

—CAROL, PRINCIPAL

❝ Schools need to have clearly defined expectations for kids. And if kids have lagging skills or unsolved problems that get in the way of meeting expectations, then we have to work to solve those problems. ❞

—TOM, ASSISTANT SUPERINTENDENT

CHAPTER 4

THE ALSUP

Identifying lagging skills (why) and unsolved problems (when) is what gets the ball rolling on effectively helping behaviorally challenging students. The instrument developed for this purpose is called the Assessment of Lagging Skills and Unsolved Problems (ALSUP). When it comes to helping behaviorally challenging kids, the ALSUP is absolutely indispensable.

Before I describe the ALSUP, let's adjust our terminology a little. We've established that doing well occurs at the interface of two forces: the expectations of the environment and the skills of the individual. When those two forces are compatible—in other words, when a student has the skills to meet certain expectations—challenging behavior does not occur. But when those two forces are incompatible—what could be referred to as the "clash of the two forces"—the likelihood of challenging behavior is heightened. Henceforth, we'll be referring to what happens when the forces clash as an *incompatibility episode*: an episode that *communicates* to us that there is incompatibility between a child's skills and certain demands and expectations.

> *An* incompatibility episode *[is] an episode that* communicates *to us that there is incompatibility between a child's skills and certain demands and expectations.*

The first thing to notice about the ALSUP (see Figure 4.1) is the list of lagging skills on the left-hand side. It's not an exhaustive list of lagging skills; if we were to be exhaustive about the skills behaviorally challenging kids have been found to be lacking, the ALSUP would be ten to fifteen pages long. We don't need ten to fifteen pages to help adults recognize that lagging skills are at the core of a student's challenging behavior, and to recognize that many of the things they've been saying about the student have been inaccurate. So it's a representative list of lagging skills. The list helps us move from the general skills of flexibility/adaptability, frustration tolerance, and problem solving to skills that are even more specific.

> To download the blank ALSUP form and the ALSUP Guide, go to www.livesinthebalance.org/LostandFound.

Down the right-hand side is where unsolved problems are documented. Again, an unsolved problem is an expectation the student is having difficulty meeting.

The fact that there is a place to check off the lagging skills can sometimes mislead people into thinking that the ALSUP is a checklist or rating scale. The ALSUP is neither a checklist nor a rating scale. Caregivers who live and work with behaviorally challenging kids are frequently asked to check and rate too much. And, of course, what we're busy checking and rating is behavior (the least important part). Then we tabulate our ratings and count our checks so that we can calculate a total score . . . then

ASSESSMENT OF LAGGING SKILLS and UNSOLVED PROBLEMS

Child's Name: _____   Date: _____

Instructions: The ALSUP is intended for use as a *discussion guide* rather than as freestanding checklist or rating scale. It should be used to identify specific lagging skills and unsolved problems that pertain to a particular child or adolescent. If a lagging skill applies, check it off and then (before moving on to the next lagging skill) identify the specific expectations the child is having difficulty meeting in association with that lagging skill (unsolved problems). A nonexhaustive list of sample unsolved problems is shown at the bottom of the page.

LAGGING SKILLS	UNSOLVED PROBLEMS
__ Difficulty handling transitions, shifting from one mind-set or task to another	
__ Difficulty doing things in a logical sequence or prescribed order	
__ Difficulty persisting on challenging or tedious tasks	
__ Poor sense of time	
__ Difficulty maintaining focus	
__ Difficulty considering the likely outcomes or consequences of actions (impulsive)	
__ Difficulty considering a range of solutions to a problem	
__ Difficulty expressing concerns, needs, or thoughts in words	
__ Difficulty understanding what is being said	
__ Difficulty managing emotional response to frustration so as to think rationally	
__ Chronic irritability and/or anxiety significantly impede capacity for problem solving or heighten frustration	
__ Difficulty seeing the "grays"/concrete, literal, black-and-white thinking	
__ Difficulty deviating from rules, routine	
__ Difficulty handling unpredictability, ambiguity, uncertainty, novelty	
__ Difficulty shifting from original idea, plan, or solution	
__ Difficulty taking into account situational factors that would suggest the need to adjust a plan of action	
__ Inflexible, inaccurate interpretations/cognitive distortions or biases (e.g., "Everyone's out to get me," "Nobody likes me," "You always blame me," "It's not fair," "I'm stupid")	
__ Difficulty attending to or accurately interpreting social cues/poor perception of social nuances	
__ Difficulty starting conversations, entering groups, connecting with people/lacking other basic social skills	
__ Difficulty seeking attention in appropriate ways	
__ Difficulty appreciating how his/her behavior is affecting other people	
__ Difficulty empathizing with others, appreciating another person's perspective or point of view	
__ Difficulty appreciating how s/he is coming across or being perceived by others	
__ Sensory/motor difficulties	

UNSOLVED PROBLEMS GUIDE: Unsolved problems are the specific expectations a child is having difficulty meeting. Unsolved problems should be free of maladaptive behavior; free of adult theories and explanations; "split" (not "clumped"); and specific.

HOME: Difficulty getting out of bed in the morning in time to get to school on time; Difficulty getting started on or completing homework (specify assignment); Difficulty ending the video game to get ready for bed at night; Difficulty coming indoors for dinner when playing outside; Difficulty agreeing with brother about what television show to watch after school; Difficulty handling the feeling of seams in socks; Difficulty brushing teeth before bedtime; Difficulty staying out of older sister's bedroom; Difficulty keeping bedroom clean; Difficulty clearing the table after dinner.
SCHOOL: Difficulty moving from choice time to math; Difficulty sitting next to Kyle during circle time; Difficulty raising hand during Social Studies discussions; Difficulty getting started on project on tectonic plates in Geography; Difficulty Standing in line for lunch; Difficulty getting along with Eduardo on the school bus; Difficulty when losing in basketball at recess

Figure 4.1: The ALSUP (Assessment of Lagging Skills and Unsolved Problems)

we compare the student's total score to normative data for kids of the same age, grade, or gender . . . all in the quest for what has become the holy grail of assessment: a *percentile* that will somehow communicate to us whether the student needs our help. But percentiles aren't very good at telling caregivers whether a student needs help or what kind of help is needed. And percentiles aren't very good at helping adults understand why and when incompatibility episodes are occurring for a particular student.

Instead, the ALSUP is a *discussion guide*—a guide for discussing a student's lagging skills and unsolved problems. Checklists don't help the different adults who are working with a student have a shared set of lenses; checklists don't help those adults speak the same language; checklists don't persuade the unpersuaded. Discussions about a student's lagging skills and unsolved problems do.

> *In meetings in which the ALSUP is the discussion guide,* the sole focus is on lagging skills and unsolved problems; *these are things we can actually do something about.*

The ALSUP helps us focus on the things we can actually do something about. Caregivers have a tendency to spend a great deal of time trying to *explain* a child's behavior, and these explanations typically center on adverse historical or environmental factors about which little can be done. These factors are frequently held up as the *cause* of a child's difficulties. Although such factors—tough neighborhoods, exposure to substances in utero, parental psychopathology, trauma, and so forth—can certainly *exacerbate* a child's difficulties, they are seldom the primary cause. In meetings in which the ALSUP is the discussion guide, *the sole focus is on lagging skills and unsolved problems*; these are things we can actually do something about. And there's no pressure to explain anything; the ALSUP is going to do the explaining for you.

USING THE ALSUP

Let's consider the format of meetings in which the ALSUP is used as the discussion guide. First, everyone in the meeting is given a *blank* copy of the ALSUP. It's actually far less productive to have participants fill out the ALSUP prior to the meeting, as that's not conducive to a discussion. And we really do want to have a discussion.

The discussion begins at the top of the ALSUP with the first lagging skill: *difficulty making transitions, shifting from one mind-set or task to another.* The assembled group is asked to consider whether that lagging skill applies to the student being discussed in the meeting. Deciding whether or not to check off a particular lagging skill isn't a democratic process: if two people feel that the student is lacking the skill and four people aren't so sure, you're still checking off that lagging skill. If the group feels that the student is not lacking that skill, you move on to the next one. But as soon as a lagging skill is checked, you're no longer moving down the list; instead you're moving *over* to identify the unsolved problems that spring to mind in association with that lagging skill. Identification of unsolved problems is prompted by the question, *"Can you give me some examples of times when [student's name] is having difficulty [repeat the lagging skill]?"* or *"Are there expectations that [student's name] is having difficulty meeting that spring to mind when you think of that lagging skill?"*

So, for example, if our expectation is that students come in from recess and back into the classroom quietly, and the student who is being discussed is having difficulty with that, then *difficulty quietly coming back into the classroom from recess* is an unsolved problem. If our expectation is that students stay in their places in line on the way from the classroom to lunch, and the student being discussed is having difficulty with that, then *difficulty staying in place in line on the way from the classroom to lunch* is an unsolved problem.

Once a lagging skill has helped us identify one unsolved problem, are we ready to move on to the next lagging skill? No, actually, *we're going to identify as many unsolved problems in association with that lagging skill as we possibly can.* When we can't think of any more, we move on to the next lagging skill. By the way, you don't want to "cherry-pick" lagging skills; it's best just to go in order. Nor do you want to waste time discussing which lagging skill best explains a given unsolved problem. You can't figure that out with great precision anyway; just assume that multiple lagging skills can contribute to the same unsolved problem.

Checking off lagging skills is the easy part of using the ALSUP. Identifying and wording unsolved problems is the hard part. There are four guidelines involved in writing unsolved problems. These guidelines make it harder to write unsolved problems, but they're worth the added difficulty, for they increase the likelihood that the student will participate in the process of solving the problem. That's because *the wording of the unsolved problem on the ALSUP translates directly into the words that will be used to introduce the problem to the child when it comes time to solve it together.* Well-worded unsolved problems get the problem-solving process off to a good start; poorly worded unsolved problems can stop the process dead in its tracks. Plus, writing unsolved problems isn't going to be hard forever; it's only going to be hard until you become comfortable with the four guidelines.

Before reviewing the guidelines, here are some key points to remember:

1. **Don't have meeting participants complete the ALSUP beforehand.** Doing so is not conducive to discussions, and it's discussions that help people speak the same language, see a child through shared lenses, and persuade the unpersuaded.
2. **Don't go down the entire list of lagging skills and then go back to think of unsolved problems.** That makes the connection between lagging skills and unsolved problems more tenuous.
3. **Don't "cherry-pick" lagging skills, bouncing from one lagging skill to another.** It's best to go in order and cover them all so that you don't miss anything.
4. **Don't identify unsolved problems and then go back to consider which lagging skill best accounts for each one.** Again, just assume that *multiple lagging skills could be contributing to the*

same unsolved problem, and it's not a good use of time to try to determine which lagging skill is the primary contributor.

5. **Identify as many unsolved problems as possible for a checked lagging skill.** *You don't need to write the same unsolved problem twice, even if a later lagging skill seems to be associated with it.* This means that, quite often, early lagging skills will have many unsolved problems written in—only because you covered them first—while later lagging skills are likely to have fewer unsolved problems.

GUIDELINES FOR WRITING UNSOLVED PROBLEMS

1. **The unsolved problem contains no challenging behaviors.** People who are unfamiliar with the ALSUP are often tempted to write challenging *behaviors* (hitting, swearing, screaming) in as the unsolved problems. But behaviors are not the unsolved problems; the unmet expectations that are causing the behaviors are the unsolved problems. Remember, behavior is just the by-product of the unsolved problem; it's the fever, the signal— it's *downstream*. The problems causing the behavior are *upstream*. So we're leaving the behavior out of the unsolved problem. In other words, we're not going to write an unsolved problem as follows: *Gets upset and runs away when told to stay in place in the line from the classroom to lunch.* "Gets upset and running away" is the behavior . . . it's gone. The unsolved problem is *Difficulty staying in place in the line from the classroom to lunch.*

> *The wording of the unsolved problem translates directly into the words you'll be using to introduce the unsolved problem to the student when it comes time to solve the problem together.*

Why is this an important guideline? Because, again, the wording of the unsolved problem translates directly into the words you'll be using to introduce the unsolved problem to the student when it comes time to solve the problem together. If you refer to a kid's challenging behavior when you're trying to solve a problem with her, she's likely to become defensive or think she's in trouble. And if one or both of those things happen, she's going to be far less receptive to participating in the discussion. And we very badly want her to participate in this discussion. Second, we want to make it crystal clear to the people in the meeting that the behavior is not the unsolved problem; again, the unmet expectation causing the behavior is the unsolved problem. That way, they'll stop talking about the behaviors and start talking about the expectations the student is having difficulty meeting.

2. **The unsolved problem contains no adult theories.**

   If we want to spend our meeting time talking about the things about which we can do something, we're going to talk a lot less (if at all) about our theories and explanations related to the cause of the student's behavior. And we're certainly not going to include theories in the wording of our unsolved problems. In other words, we wouldn't write *Difficulty sitting next to Thomas during circle time because her parents are going through a very difficult divorce* as an unsolved problem. Anything that comes after the word *because* is pretty much guaranteed to be a theory and is left out of the unsolved problem.

   Why? First, even though school meetings have traditionally been the venue in which adults try to explain a child's behavior, *our theories are often wrong.* We think they're right, but they're wrong a lot more often than we think they are. Again, when you're using the ALSUP, there's no pressure to explain anything. You're focused solely on identifying lagging skills and unsolved problems. Second, as you know, the wording of the unsolved problem is going to translate directly into the wording we use to introduce the problem to the kid when the time comes to solve the problem together. Throwing a theory at the kid when you really want to talk about the unsolved problem—*"I've noticed you're having difficulty sitting next to Thomas during circle time because your parents are going through a very difficult divorce"*—is likely to confuse the kid and make it very difficult for her to figure out what information you're seeking (*"Are they asking me about sitting next to Thomas or about the divorce?"*). Many will simply say, *"I don't know,"* or not respond at all.

Along these lines, I've begun recommending that adults strive for something I call *assumption-free living.* The minute one begins assuming that one already understands what's making it hard for a kid to meet a given expectation, one should get rid of that assumption as quickly as possible. It's just a distraction. Plus, as you'll soon see, it's much more reliable to simply ask the kid.

Having school staff talk about lagging skills and unsolved problems instead of theories is a very productive development. Hard in the beginning, but very productive.

3. **The unsolved problem is split, not clumped.**
What does this mean? Here are some examples of clumped unsolved problems:

- Difficulty getting along with others
- Difficulty reading
- Difficulty staying safe
- Difficulty following directions
- Difficulty listening
- Difficulty doing as told
- Difficulty writing

Let's use that last one to clarify. If we use the words, *"I've noticed you're having difficulty writing"* to introduce an unsolved problem, then we're asking the student to think about *all* of the different assignments she's having difficulty writing and *all* of the different reasons she's having difficulty writing them. That's often asking for too much sorting through, so such wording greatly increases the likelihood of the student responding with *"I don't know."* Plus, while it's tempting to believe that the student is having difficulty on all of the writing assignments for the *exact same reason*, that won't actually be the case most of the time.

So we're going to *split* the unsolved problem by being precise about the specific individual writing tasks and assignments the student is having difficulty completing. Let's say she's having difficulty writing the term paper in social studies, difficulty writing the definitions to the spelling words in English, and difficulty writing the answers to the word problems in math. Those are three separate unsolved problems.

Our motto is *split early; maybe you can clump later . . . but if you clump early, you'll never find out.* This means that when it comes time to solve problems collaboratively, we're going to talk to the student about *one* of the writing tasks or assignments she's having difficulty completing (say, *difficulty completing the term paper in social studies*). Because it's been split, we've greatly increased the likelihood that she will participate in the discussion and provide us with information. After we're through gathering information from the student about that single writing task or assignment, we can then ask her if what we now understand about the reasons she's having difficulty completing the term paper in social studies also helps us understand the difficulty she's having in writing the definitions to the spelling words in English. The answer is either yes or no. If the answer is no, it's good that we split the unsolved problem, because the student's difficulties on the two writing assignments are different. But even if the answer is yes, splitting was still a smart play, because the student would have been less likely to talk about it if it had been clumped.

One of the biggest concerns people have about splitting unsolved problems is that it makes the list of unsolved problems very long. But a long list of unsolved problems represents the reality. If there are many expectations the student is having difficulty meeting, then we're not doing her or ourselves any favors by pretending that the list is shorter than it really is. The real favor is that, finally at long last, all of the expectations the student has been having difficulty meeting for a very long time have been identified. Plus, even if the list is lengthy, you're not going to be working on all of the unsolved problems at once anyway. We'll discuss prioritizing later in this chapter.

4. **The unsolved problem is specific.**

There are two strategies that will help make the unsolved problem as specific as possible:

> **Strategy 1:** asking "W questions" (*who, what, where,* and *when,* but not *why*)
> **Strategy 2:** inquiring about the expectation the student is actually having difficulty meeting

Examples

Let's bring these strategies to life with some examples. Let's say the meeting participants want to write *"Difficulty being impulsive"* as an unsolved problem. First, that's a lagging skill, not an unsolved problem. (You'll find impulsiveness in the list of lagging skills.) Remember, the unsolved problems would be the specific expectations a student is having difficulty meeting that spring to mind in association with poor impulse control. So now let's use our strategies.

Where is she impulsive? (Strategy 1)
>   *"She's impulsive during social studies."*

What's going on during social studies when she's being impulsive? (Strategy 1)
>   *"She always calls out answers without raising her hand during social studies discussions."*

That unsolved problem just became a lot more specific after just two applications of Strategy 1. We're almost ready to log that unsolved problem on the ALSUP. But it needs a little additional refining, because there's still a challenging behavior (calling out answers) in there. Let's take *calling out answers* out of the unsolved problem and insert the word *difficulty*. Now we have an unsolved problem (*Difficulty raising hand during social studies discussions*) that contains no challenging behavior, contains no adult theories, is split, and is specific.

You might be thinking that "raising hand" is a behavior, and you'd be right, but it's not a *challenging* behavior. It's the expectation that the student is having difficulty meeting, so it's fine.

Here's another example. Let's say the group has decided that a student "has a lot of rage." Not good, right? That's either a behavior or a theory, but it's not a specific unsolved problem (yet). So let's use our strategies:

<u>Where</u> does she have a lot of rage? (Strategy 1)
  "Recess."
<u>What's</u> going on during recess—and with <u>whom</u>—that makes you
  say she has a lot of rage? (Strategy 1)
  *"She always kicks her best friend, Teresa, when they disagree about the
  rules in the four-square game."*

That's a lot more specific. We're almost ready to write that unsolved problem down on the ALSUP. There's only one problem with that unsolved problem: there's a challenging behavior in there (kicking). So let's take *kicking* out and put the word *difficulty* in. Now what do we have? *Difficulty agreeing with Teresa on the rules in the four-square game during recess.*

Let's try one more. Let's say a meeting participant proposes *"Difficulty with the word no"* as the unsolved problem. Don't write that in! The word *no* is not the unsolved problem. What caregivers are saying "no" about could be the unsolved problem. Let's use our strategies:

<u>What</u> are you saying no about? (Strategy 1)
  *"I'm saying, 'No, you can't go to the bathroom eighteen times during
  every math period.'"*

OK, well, going to the bathroom a lot during math period is the behavior . . . but <u>what expectation is she having difficulty meeting</u> during math period? (Strategy 2)
> *"Oh, she's having difficulty completing the division problems on the worksheet during math."*

<u>What</u> is she having trouble with on the division on the worksheet? (Strategy 1)
> *"Double-digit division problems."*

So are you saying that she's having difficulty completing the double-digit division problems on the worksheet during math?
> *"Yes!"*

Difficulty completing the double-digit division problems on the worksheet during math is the unsolved problem.

Here are some examples of unsolved problems that do not meet the guidelines. Try to figure out which guideline the unsolved problem isn't meeting.

Difficulty moving from one assignment to the next.

If you recognized that this is clumped, well done! To split it, we'd need to be more explicit about the specific assignments the student is having difficulty moving from and to, even if that means writing ten different unsolved problems. Strategy 1 (<u>What</u> *assignments is she having difficulty moving from and to?*) should help. Some examples of split unsolved problems that might be identified in this instance:

Difficulty moving from English to math.
Difficulty moving from recess back into the classroom.
Difficulty moving from the resource room back to the classroom for math.

Again, while it would be tempting to think that the student is having difficulty moving from all assignments, classes, and activities to the next for the exact same reason, that's unlikely to be true. Here's another:

Difficulty moving from a preferred activity to a less preferred activity.

Clumped, yes? And now we've added a very common theory (preferred and less preferred). We're a lot better off just documenting the specific activities the student is having difficulty moving from and to (using Strategy 1):

Difficulty moving from lunch to the resource room.
Difficulty coming from the bus into the classroom in the morning.

Here's another:

Difficulty completing difficult assignments.

This, you may have noticed, is clumped and may also contain a theory. What we really want to identify are the specific assignments the student is having difficulty completing (using Strategy 1):

Difficulty completing the word problems on the worksheet in math.
Difficulty getting started on the definitions in English.
Difficulty getting started on the geography project in history.

Here's another:

Difficulty treating others with respect when she's upset.

Now, this one is pointing us downstream (*when she's upset*). To make this unsolved problem more specific, we'd need to ask about the problems that are causing the student to become upset (Strategy 1). Ultimately, it's those unsolved problems that would take the place of the original:

Difficulty finding someone to sit with at lunch.

Difficulty finding someone to sit with on the school bus.

Difficulty when she thinks the kids are cheating during the four-square game at recess.

How do you know that last one isn't a theory? Whenever a potential theory is raised in an ALSUP discussion, you'll want to ask the informant, *"How sure are you?"* If the answer is, *"Not very sure,"* it's probably a theory. But if the informant responds, *"She [the student] has told me that's why she gets upset at recess,"* it's no theory.

In other words, information that's already been provided by the student is usually good protection against adult theorizing. But it's not infallible. A long time ago, I asked a four-year-old girl why she was exhibiting challenging behavior (that's a question I wouldn't ask anymore), and she responded, "I do it for negative reinforcement." Because most kids that age aren't familiar with the concept of negative reinforcement, it was a distinct possibility that the girl was restating a theory that had been provided to her by adults, and additional querying confirmed this.

Here's another:

Difficulty when Mrs. Thomas says she's lost recess.

This one refers to a punishment that is being applied *after* a student exhibits a behavior that is resulting from an unsolved problem that isn't specified; so now we're *way* downstream. Neither the behavior nor the punishment is the unsolved problem. So let's paddle upstream:

<u>What</u> is she losing recess for? (Strategy 1)

  "Talking to her classmates during math."

<u>What expectation is she having difficulty meeting</u> when she's talking to her classmates during math? (Strategy 2)

*"Well, she's not supposed to be talking to them . . . and she's not com-
    pleting her word problems."*
So she's having difficulty completing the word problems during
    math?
*"Yes . . . and she's having difficulty remaining quiet during work time
    in math."*
Good . . . so we have two unsolved problems there, yes?
"Yes."

Here's yet another:

Difficulty accepting help.

Clumped, yes? We'd want to know the specific assignments
the student needs help with; those are the unsolved problems.
Also, you'll want to stay away from the word "accepting" (often
what the student is having difficulty "accepting" is an adult-
imposed solution, which is downstream).

<u>What</u> is it that you want her to accept help with? (Strategy 1)
    "Writing paragraphs in Writer's Workshop."
<u>What expectation is she having difficulty meeting</u> in writing the
    paragraphs in Writer's Workshop? (Strategy 2)
    "Adding details."
So she's having difficulty adding the details to the paragraphs
    during Writer's Workshop?
    "Yes."

Here's still another:

Difficulty staying focused due to socializing with her friends.

This one contains situationally challenging behavior (socializing with friends). It's also clumped; we'd want to know what tasks
the student is having difficulty completing. We also want to stay

away from words like "focused," as we really have no way of knowing whether the student is actually focused or not (but we do know the tasks the student is having difficulty completing). In addition, the wording of the lagging skill really shouldn't find its way into the unsolved problem.

<u>When</u> is that happening? (Strategy 1)
> *"All the time."*

But more specifically <u>when</u>? (Strategy 1)
> *"You mean an example of a time when that happens?"*

Yes, please.
> *"Geography."*

And <u>what expectation is she having difficulty meeting</u> during geography that makes you say she's not focused and too busy socializing with her friends? (Strategy 2)
> *"Well, she's not getting her work done."*

<u>What</u> work? (Strategy 1)
> *"Well, right now we're working on the map of Africa."*

So she's having difficulty completing the map of Africa in geography?
> *"Yes."*

Just a few more:

Difficulty arriving to class on time.
> Clumped. <u>What</u> class(es)?

Difficulty doing things on the first request.
> Clumped. <u>What</u> things?

Difficulty if things don't go her way.
> Clumped. Also possibly a theory. <u>What</u> things?

Difficulty not lying.
> Pure behavior. What's the student lying about? Some people might be tempted to change this to *Difficulty telling the truth*, and that might feel like a step in the right direction, but it's still clumped, and we'd still need to know what the

student is having difficulty telling the truth about. If the student is having difficulty telling the truth about whether she's completed her lab reports in science, then *Difficulty not lying* and *Difficulty telling the truth*—which are downstream—would be replaced by *Difficulty completing her lab reports in science.*

Also, you want to avoid unsolved problems that include the word *not* whenever possible, especially as the *not* often refers to a challenging behavior. So *Difficulty not pushing people in the lunch line* would be altered to the actual expectation the student is having difficulty meeting: *Difficulty keeping hands to self in the lunch line.* And *Difficulty not calling kids mean names on the bus* would be altered to *Difficulty speaking kindly to John and Trevor on the school bus.*

Here's one more:

Difficulty getting off the computer when I tell her to.
> The *difficulty getting off the computer* part is fine, but the *when I tell her to* part isn't, mostly because it's not specific enough.
> So let's ask some questions:

When are you telling her to get off the computer?
> *"At the end of choice time."*

And what expectation is she having difficulty meeting when she doesn't turn off the computer at the end of choice time?
> *"She's supposed to be going to math."*

Always math?
> *"Yes, math is always after choice time."*

So she's having difficulty turning off the computer at the end of choice time to go to math?
> *"Yes!"*

Enough examples of what could go wrong and how to get it right? OK, here's an example of an ALSUP reflecting well-worded unsolved problems (Figure 4.2).

ASSESSMENT OF LAGGING SKILLS and UNSOLVED PROBLEMS

Child's Name: _____ Date: _____

Instructions: The ALSUP is intended for use as a *discussion guide* rather than as freestanding checklist or rating scale. It should be used to identify specific lagging skills and unsolved problems that pertain to a particular child or adolescent. If a lagging skill applies, check it off and then (before moving on to the next lagging skill) identify the specific expectations the child is having difficulty meeting in association with that lagging skill (unsolved problems). A nonexhaustive list of sample unsolved problems is shown at the bottom of the page.

LAGGING SKILLS	UNSOLVED PROBLEMS
✔ Difficulty handling transitions, shifting from one mind-set or task to another	Difficulty moving from homeroom to Chinese class
✔ Difficulty doing things in a logical sequence or prescribed order	Difficulty keeping hands to self in the hallway between Geography and World History
✔ Difficulty persisting on challenging or tedious tasks	Difficulty keeping hands to self in the hallway between World History and Math
__ Poor sense of time	Difficulty getting to school on time
__ Difficulty maintaining focus	Difficulty turning in vocabulary homework in Chinese
✔ Difficulty considering the likely outcomes or consequences of actions (impulsive)	Difficulty putting away iPhone during homeroom
✔ Difficulty considering a range of solutions to a problem	Difficulty getting along with Geoff during football in physical education
__ Difficulty expressing concerns, needs, or thoughts in words	Difficulty completing the reading assignments for homework in American Literature
__ Difficulty understanding what is being said	Difficulty participating in class discussions in American Literature
✔ Difficulty managing emotional response to frustration so as to think rationally	Difficulty sitting next to Geoff during American Literature
__ Chronic irritability and/or anxiety significantly impede capacity for problem solving or heighten frustration	Difficulty getting along with Geoff on the school bus
__ Difficulty seeing the "grays"/concrete, literal, black-and-white thinking	Difficulty standing in line next to Tucker waiting for the bus after school
__ Difficulty deviating from rules, routine	Difficulty standing in line next to Tucker in the lunch line
__ Difficulty handling unpredictability, ambiguity, uncertainty, novelty	Difficulty getting along with Tucker during lunch
__ Difficulty shifting from original idea, plan, or solution	Difficulty copying lab information from the board during Biology
✔ Difficulty taking into account situational factors that would suggest the need to adjust a plan of action	Difficulty remaining in the classroom during Biology
__ Inflexible, inaccurate interpretations/cognitive distortions or biases (e.g., "Everyone's out to get me," "Nobody likes me," "You always blame me, "It's not fair," "I'm stupid")	Difficulty writing homework assignments into planner
__ Difficulty attending to or accurately interpreting social cues/poor perception of social nuances	Difficulty taking planner home at the end of the school day
__ Difficulty starting conversations, entering groups, connecting with people/lacking other basic social skills	
__ Difficulty seeking attention in appropriate ways	
✔ Difficulty appreciating how his/her behavior is affecting other people	
✔ Difficulty empathizing with others, appreciating another person's perspective or point of view	
✔ Difficulty appreciating how s/he is coming across or being perceived by others	
__ Sensory/motor difficulties	

UNSOLVED PROBLEMS GUIDE: Unsolved problems are the specific expectations a child is having difficulty meeting. Unsolved problems should be free of maladaptive behavior; free of adult theories and explanations; "split" (not "clumped"); and specific.

HOME: Difficulty getting out of bed in the morning in time to get to school on time; Difficulty getting started on or completing homework (specify assignment); Difficulty ending the video game to get ready for bed at night; Difficulty coming indoors for dinner when playing outside; Difficulty agreeing with brother about what television show to watch after school; Difficulty handling the feeling of seams in socks; Difficulty brushing teeth before bedtime; Difficulty staying out of older sister's bedroom; Difficulty keeping bedroom clean; Difficulty clearing the table after dinner.
SCHOOL: Difficulty moving from choice time to math; Difficulty sitting next to Kyle during circle time; Difficulty raising hand during Social Studies discussions; Difficulty getting started on project on tectonic plates in Geography; Difficulty Standing in line for lunch; Difficulty getting along with Eduardo on the school bus; Difficulty when losing in basketball at recess

Figure 4.2: A Completed ALSUP

Productive Meetings

Aside from identifying lagging skills and unsolved problems, what do we hope happens in an ALSUP meeting? A whole bunch of good things:

- Participants come to appreciate that the student is, indeed, lacking a lot of skills, so they're now wearing—or, at least, trying on for size—different lenses.
- Participants come to appreciate why interventions that have been focused primarily on motivation haven't been working. Motivation wasn't the issue all along.
- Participants who have been treating the student in a harsh, adversarial, punitive manner may start to feel some regret now that they understand what's really getting in the way for the student.
- Participants come to recognize that incompatibility episodes occur only in the context of specific unsolved problems, and are therefore highly predictable.
- Participants also come to recognize that if those problems are solved, they won't cause incompatibility episodes anymore.
- Participants recognize that if unsolved problems are predictable, they can be solved proactively rather than emergently.

If those things are accomplished in a meeting, then participants will leave the meeting with new lenses (lagging skills), a new language, and a clear sense of what problems need to be solved. The alternative, of course, is to continue discussing behaviors, diagnoses, and things about which nothing can be done, in which case participants will continue to leave meetings feeling that they can do nothing to help the student, and also possibly feeling that the meeting was a complete waste of time.

You may have noticed that the student is not present in the ALSUP meeting. Although we want to be collaborating with the student on solving problems as soon as possible, we need to facilitate the free flow of information among school staff in discussing the student's lagging skills and unsolved problems before the problem solving begins. If the student is present, staff might not feel at liberty to speak freely, and there's always the risk of the student disagreeing with what the staff are saying. So the student isn't present at this meeting. But that doesn't mean the student doesn't have valuable information to offer, especially in the realm of unsolved problems. Thus it's a good idea to meet separately with the student for the purpose of gathering this information. Because students aren't familiar with your new terminology, you wouldn't ask a student about her unsolved problems. But you could ask, *"What are people bugging you about?"* (whatever people are bugging her about must be an unsolved problem or they wouldn't be bugging her about it); or *"What are people giving you a hard time about?"* (again, whatever people are giving her a hard time about must be an unsolved problem or they wouldn't be giving her a hard time about it); or *"What are you getting in trouble for?"* (students don't get in trouble over solved problems; they only get into trouble over unsolved problems). Any new unsolved problems provided by the student should be added to the list on the ALSUP.

Prioritizing

A few things can happen after you've identified a student's lagging skills and unsolved problems. One possibility is that you may feel completely overwhelmed by the realization that there is a monumental task at hand. Behaviorally challenging students often have quite a few lagging skills. And, if you've done a good job of splitting, a given student may have thirty to forty different unsolved problems.

There's a silver lining to all those lagging skills and unsolved problems: *at least you now know what they are.* In other words, *not* knowing about them is far more overwhelming than knowing about them. And you're not going to be trying to solve all of those unsolved problems at once anyway, tempting as that might be. Indeed, trying to solve all of those problems at once is the best way to ensure that none of them get solved at all.

You're going to have to prioritize. Which unsolved problems are going to be solved first, and which are we setting aside for now?

> *Now you don't have to wait until the student disrupts*
> *the class before you try to solve the problem that causes the*
> *disruption; you can do it in advance because the problem*
> *(and the disruption) are predictable.*

Before we talk about that, here's another reason to feel less overwhelmed by that long list of unsolved problems: now that you've identified them, they can be solved *proactively*. When unsolved problems remain unidentified, you're still stuck trying to deal with them emergently and reactively, and that's just a lot less effective. Now you don't have to wait until the student disrupts the class before you try to solve the problem that causes the disruption; you can do it in advance because the problem (and the disruption) are predictable. In other words, you're no longer responding to one incident after another (an approach captured by the well-known maxim related to chickens with their heads cut off). You're solving the problems that are causing those incidents, and now you know what those problems are. Your head is very much on.

And what about all those lagging skills you've checked off? Don't they have to be taught? Well, yes and no. Yes, improving those skills would be a very positive development. But you're actually not going to be teaching the vast majority of skills on the ALSUP in a direct or explicit manner *because there's no technology for doing so*. True, some of the skills—some basic social skills and language processing and communication skills—can be taught directly, and there you'd want to rely on programs such as Michelle Garcia-Winner's Social Thinking model. But the vast majority of skills are going to be taught *indirectly*, by solving problems collaboratively and proactively. Put another way, *when you're solving problems collaboratively and proactively, you're simultaneously (but indirectly) teaching the student the skills she's lacking*.

So your primary focal point is the unsolved problems. Which ones should you prioritize? First and foremost, any that are causing safety issues. If there are no safety issues, go with the unsolved problems that are causing incompatibility episodes with the greatest frequency. But don't obsess over prioritizing; getting started with the process of solving problems collaboratively and proactively is more important than splitting hairs over which specific unsolved problems to start with. Can the student help you decide which unsolved problems to prioritize? Sure, why not?

How many unsolved problems should you target initially? No more than three. Any more than that, and both you and the student will be working on too many things at once. What are you doing with the rest? You're setting them aside, at least for now. Unsolved problems that have been removed from the agenda won't set in motion incompatibility episodes anymore. You'll read more about the setting aside part in later chapters.

How do you keep track of everything? With another instrument—also a single-sided, single sheet of paper—called the Problem Solving Plan (Figure 4.3). This instrument provides a convenient mechanism for listing the problems that are presently prioritized for a student, designating the person who's taking primary responsibility for solving that problem with the student, and tracking progress in solving the problem. Once a problem is solved, it is removed from the Problem Solving Plan and another problem from the ALSUP takes its place. (See Figure 4.4 for a filled-out Problem Solving Plan.)

To download the Problem Solving Plan form, go to www.livesinthebalance.org/LostandFound.

Some schools have found that the Problem Solving Plan eventually takes the place of the old Behavior Plan. The Behavior Plan is focused on the wrong thing (behaviors); the Problem Solving Plan is focused on the right thing (the problems that are causing those behaviors).

PROBLEM SOLVING PLAN
(PLAN B FLOWCHART)

Child's Name _____ Date _____

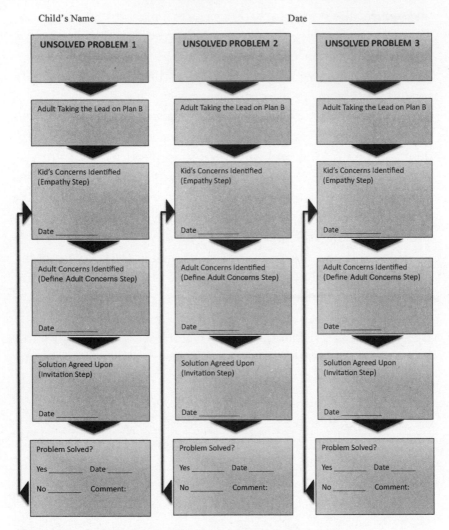

Figure 4.3: Problem Solving Plan (Plan B Flowchart)

Why is it important to designate the adult who's taking primary responsibility for solving a given problem with the student? Because if no one is designated, one of two bad things will happen. Possibility number one: everyone will work on the problem with the student, which is both overkill and unlikely. Possibility

PROBLEM SOLVING PLAN
(PLAN B FLOWCHART)

Child's Name _____ Date _____

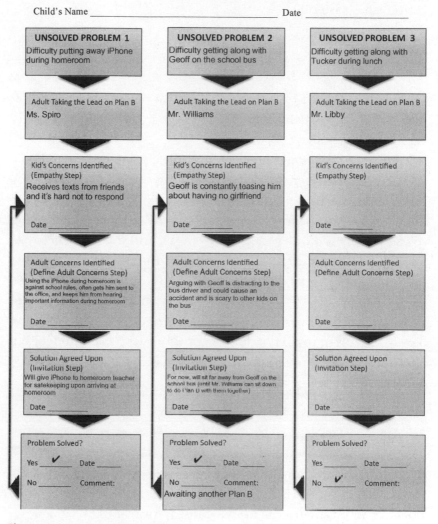

UNSOLVED PROBLEM 1
Difficulty putting away iPhone during homeroom

Adult Taking the Lead on Plan B
Ms. Spiro

Kid's Concerns Identified (Empathy Step)
Receives texts from friends and it's hard not to respond

Date _____

Adult Concerns Identified (Define Adult Concerns Step)
Using the iPhone during homeroom is against school rules, often gets him sent to the office, and keeps him from hearing important information during homeroom

Date _____

Solution Agreed Upon (Invitation Step)
Will give iPhone to homeroom teacher for safekeeping upon arriving at homeroom

Date _____

Problem Solved?

Yes ✔ Date _____

No _____ Comment:

UNSOLVED PROBLEM 2
Difficulty getting along with Geoff on the school bus

Adult Taking the Lead on Plan B
Mr. Williams

Kid's Concerns Identified (Empathy Step)
Geoff is constantly teasing him about having no girlfriend

Date _____

Adult Concerns Identified (Define Adult Concerns Step)
Arguing with Geoff is distracting to the bus driver and could cause an accident and is scary to other kids on the bus

Date _____

Solution Agreed Upon (Invitation Step)
For now, will sit far away from Geoff on the school bus (until Mr. Williams can sit down to do Plan B with them together)

Date _____

Problem Solved?

Yes ✔ Date _____

No _____ Comment:
Awaiting another Plan B

UNSOLVED PROBLEM 3
Difficulty getting along with Tucker during lunch

Adult Taking the Lead on Plan B
Mr. Libby

Kid's Concerns Identified (Empathy Step)

Date _____

Adult Concerns Identified (Define Adult Concerns Step)

Date _____

Solution Agreed Upon (Invitation Step)

Date _____

Problem Solved?

Yes _____ Date _____

No ✔ Comment:

Figure 4.4: A Completed PSP

number two (more likely): no one will work on the problem with the student, in which case the problem will remain unsolved.

In the hustle and bustle of the school day, problems (and students) can get lost in the shuffle. Under such circumstances, the problems never get identified and solved. The ALSUP and

Problem Solving Plan keep that from happening. They keep things organized. They make problem solving systematic and pro-active. They save time.

Q & A

Question: What if I have thirty students in my classroom and five or ten of them are behaviorally challenging? Do I need an ALSUP for all of the challenging ones?

   Answer: That would be ideal, just to help you organize the effort. Helping ten behaviorally challenging students is a daunting task in and of itself, and it's even more daunting if you're not going about it in a systematic, planned manner. Remember, all those unsolved problems didn't get there overnight, and you're not going to get them solved overnight either. So, rather than chronically putting out brushfires—let's face it, that's why those problems got stacked up in the first place—you'll know what problems you're trying to solve (and which ones you're not prioritizing) with each student. Slowly but surely, you'll not only see progress with each student but also in the general functioning of your class as a whole.

Question: For the less challenging kids, do I need a complete ALSUP, or can I just start solving problems?

   Answer: You can solve a problem collaboratively with a student whenever you want. But if a student has a long list of unsolved problems, the organizing and prioritizing piece is critical. Otherwise you run the risk of working on everything at once, or of working on problems that aren't your top priorities.

Question: Is the student's parent present at the ALSUP meeting?

   Answer: No, not usually at the first one. The free flow of information is the premium, and school staff may not speak freely in the presence of the student's parent. Better to ask the parent(s) about the student's lagging skills and unsolved problems in a separate meeting.

Question: In my school, we don't really meet together as a group very often. Is the ALSUP something I can complete on my own?

Answer: Yes, you could complete the ALSUP on your own. But better to find ways to get together with all the people in the building who interact with the child. That way, everyone's on the same page. Helping all the adults who interact with the child get on the same page regarding lenses and priorities is crucial. And the expectations the student is having difficulty meeting may vary from one adult to another.

Question: What if, in a meeting, when I'm probing for specific unsolved problems after checking off a lagging skill, the participants respond with "always" or "with everyone"?

Answer: Use the two strategies you just read about to transform those responses into specific unsolved problems. Here's what that might sound like:

FACILITATOR: *Does Zoe have difficulty making transitions?*

PARTICIPANT: *Oh, absolutely.*

FACILITATOR: *OK, let's check that off. When does she have difficulty making transitions?*

PARTICIPANT: *All the time.*

FACILITATOR: *Well, like with who?*

PARTICIPANT: *Everybody.*

FACILITATOR: *Where?*

PARTICIPANT: *Everywhere.*

FACILITATOR: *Can you give me an example of a transition she had difficulty making yesterday?*

PARTICIPANT: *Oh, well, she had difficulty coming back into the classroom from recess yesterday.*

FACILITATOR: *Is that something she often has difficulty doing?*

PARTICIPANT: *Definitely.*

FACILITATOR: *So, it sounds like Difficulty coming back into the classroom from recess is one of our unsolved problems, yes?*

PARTICIPANT: *Yes! Now I see what you're after.*

Question: What if it takes more than one meeting to cover all the lagging skills and unsolved problems?

Answer: That'll be time well spent, especially when we consider how much time is being spent on the student because we haven't yet identified her lagging skills and unsolved problems.

Question: Isn't there something to be said for letting staff vent about students in a meeting?

Answer: Sure, for about two minutes. But if the entire meeting is spent on venting—if staff never get around to the information (lagging skills and unsolved problems) that will help them do something about the behaviors they're venting about—then they'll still be venting in the next meeting . . . and the next.

Question: On previous iterations of the ALSUP, weren't the lagging skills divided into categories?

Answer: Yes, quite some time ago, the lagging skills were divided into five categories: executive skills, language processing and communication skills, emotion regulation skills, cognitive flexibility skills, and social skills. But I found that the categories were doing more harm than good. First, there's so much overlap among the categories that it's actually a bit artificial to treat them as discrete entities. Second, I found that caregivers were counting the number of checks within a category as a means of prioritizing, when it's actually not lagging skills that are being prioritized; it's unsolved problems that are being prioritized. Third, it's the specific lagging skills—not the categories—that really help caregivers understand what's getting in the way for a kid.

Question: Aren't lagging skills and unsolved problems kind of negative? Isn't it important to focus on the student's strengths too?

Answer: It's great to focus on a kid's strengths in addition to her lagging skills and unsolved problems. Remember, though, that it's not the strengths that are contributing to incompatibility episodes; it's lagging skills and unsolved problems. And although talking about lagging skills and unsolved problems may seem negative, it's a vast improvement over what caregivers have been saying about a behaviorally challenging kid. Interestingly, the CPS model is usually characterized as a strength-based approach.

Question: In talking about unmet expectations, is it also useful to think about whether the expectations are realistic for the student?

Answer: That's a very important part of the discussion. Unrealistic expectations are often a major precipitant of incompatibility episodes.

Question: I can see completing the ALSUP and Problem Solving Plan in the usual meetings that take place in my school. But where do you think I'm going to find the time to solve all of those problems?

Answer: There are some pockets of time throughout the school day that can be devoted to problem solving if we're systematic about it. Before school, after school, during lunch, during recess, during prep time, when the rest of the class is busy working on something—these are all times that can be devoted to problem solving. And, as you'll read in chapter 8, many schools have committed to carving out specific times every day to solving problems with students. Not solving problems takes up a lot more time than solving them.

> *Not solving problems takes up a lot more time than solving them.*

EXPERIENCE IS THE BEST TEACHER

❝Having worked with many teachers to support them in completing an ALSUP, I am always amazed at their reaction the first time we sit down and do it together. As they check off lagging skills, you can observe and feel them developing a deeper understanding of why some of the maladaptive behaviors are occurring. Once that process begins, they are much more able to focus on the problems instead of the symptoms. They truly start to understand the student, and the empathy and approach that results from that understanding are critical to reaching the student and helping her solve problems collaboratively."

—Ryan, assistant principal

"Doing the ALSUP before starting to solve problems is really important. Otherwise, you don't know what problems you're solving.**"**

—Susan, principal

"If you jump into solving problems and you haven't really done the ALSUP first, you're kind of putting the cart before the horse.**"**

—Carol, principal

"The splitting part is really important too. If you try to solve clumped problems, they're too big and they don't get solved. My expression is, 'Solve one or you solve none.'**"**

—Tom, assistant superintendent

"We struggled with the ALSUP in the beginning. We were taking way too long. There was still way too much hypothesizing and theorizing going on in our meetings, and it was really hard to get away from that because that's what the teachers wanted to talk about. But once we got rid of all that chatter, we could usually get an ALSUP done in fifty minutes.**"**

—Susan, principal

"These days, if I'm sitting in a meeting and all they're doing is theorizing and talking about behavior and telling stories, I get frustrated and bored. I feel like, 'This is so pointless. We're not talking about anything that we can change.' All the theorizing can *feel* productive because we're talking about the kid, we're making connections, we're talking about her life. But then you realize there's no point in talking about that stuff. Let's talk about things we can actually do something about.**"**

—Katie, learning center teacher

"On our first ALSUP, the student had a lot of lagging skills and unsolved problems. But we sorted through them all and then we decided what we were going to work on first. We started with two unsolved problems involving writing, because that was particularly hard for him. And we had another related to coming into the building in the morning. And we noticed that once those problems were solved, she was much more comfortable talking with us. It got to the point where we didn't even need to prompt her to talk with us because she would come to us on her own and say, 'I really need to talk with you' or 'I really need to tell you something.'"

—KATHY, SECOND-GRADE TEACHER

"Sometimes, due to time, specialists (music, art, and so forth) and paraprofessionals can get left out of the conversation in schools. Including them in ALSUP meetings is so valuable. They have so much insight, and I think we forget about that sometimes because they have such a hard schedule. They have such an important voice because they see everybody in the whole school."

—NINA, PRINCIPAL

"You know, in the old days, when we'd get together to meet about a kid, all the people who worked with the kid in the school would get together to talk about everything we knew about the kid and then brainstorm solutions. And the teacher would choose two or three to try. Now we know someone was missing from the problem-solving process: the student. Now we only really talk about lagging skills and unsolved problems in our meetings, because we can't come up with solutions without knowing the kid's concerns and without involving the kid in the solution."

—KATHY, SECOND-GRADE TEACHER

"You're not only prioritizing unsolved problems; you're prioritizing students as well. Many schools have a lot of behaviorally challenging students, and it can be overwhelming to think of helping them all simultaneously. In the beginning, you're just choosing a few kids and a few unsolved problems to work with, especially if you're new to the model. Trying to jump in the deep end right off the bat can be a bit discouraging."

—CAROL, PRINCIPAL

❝ You have to accept that you have no control over a student's home life. You only can control what's going on at school. And if something happens at school and we expect parents to deal with it, we don't know if it's going to be dealt with or not. So what happens at school needs to be dealt with at school. ❞

—KATHY, SECOND-GRADE TEACHER

❝ What struck me as I began using the ALSUP was how much we adults were focused on our theories about the factors that were causing our students to have difficulty. We'd compete with each other to see who had the most insight about the kid. We were totally focused on things like gang affiliation, family problems, protective services, suspension histories, probation cases, and psychiatric diagnosis. It's not that these things are irrelevant, it's just that we found it hard to take these theories and turn them into plans for changing our student's lives. In fact, the more we theorized, the more powerless we felt to help the student make any progress. The stakes are so high for our students, and there's always the feeling that we can't intervene quickly enough to prevent real tragedy. When we started learning the ALSUP, we discovered the unsolved problems that had been causing great difficulty for our students—and that had remained unsolved—for a very long time. We discovered that we'd been focused on the wrong things. ❞

—ANONYMOUS SCHOOL PRINCIPAL

❧

CHAPTER 5

THE PLANS

Now that we've used the ALSUP to identify a student's lagging skills, we've answered the question *why*. Good that we're viewing the student's behavioral challenges through progressive lenses. And now that we've used the ALSUP to identify the student's unsolved problems, we've answered the question *when*. Good that we're quite clear about the task at hand. And now that we've used the Problem Solving Plan to prioritize, we know which unsolved problems we'll be trying to solve first and the ones we're setting aside for now. Good that we know what we're working on. We're now ready to start thinking about our options. There are basically three options for dealing with unsolved problems, and they're called Plan A, Plan B, and Plan C.

Plan A refers to solving a problem *unilaterally*, typically through the *imposition of adult will*. Plan A is far and away the most popular way that adults handle problems or unmet expectations with kids, and not only in schools. Its popularity notwithstanding, Plan A can actually be counterproductive in many ways and, for a variety of reasons, isn't the ideal approach to solving problems. More on that in a few paragraphs.

Plan C involves *setting aside* a particular unsolved problem, at least temporarily. Don't worry, Plan C is not the equivalent of giving in or capitulating. There's no such thing as giving in or capitulating in the CPS model. There is, however, such a thing as *prioritizing* in the CPS model, and, as you've read, prioritizing is actually a crucial aspect of organizing our efforts to help behaviorally challenging students.

Plan B involves solving a problem *collaboratively*. It's Plan B that helps you create a partnership with the student. It has the greatest potential for durably solving problems, helps you engage the student in solving the problems that affect his life, and simultaneously (but indirectly) teaches the student the skills he's lacking.

> *The Plans are purely for the expectations a student is having* difficulty *meeting.*

By the way, if a student is meeting a given expectation, you don't need a Plan. It's not an unsolved problem. The Plans are purely for the expectations a student is having *difficulty* meeting.

The Plans provide a nice framework—a shorthand—for considering how we're approaching unsolved problems. If you're trying to solve a problem, you're using either Plan A, Plan B, or Plan C. Let's take a closer look at each option.

PLAN A

If a kid isn't meeting a given expectation, one way to solve the problem is by imposing a solution. The words *"I've decided that..."* tell you that's exactly what you're doing, as in, "Because you're having difficulty keeping your hands to yourself in line when we're walking to recess, *I've decided that* you'll be walking next to me in the back of the line from now on." Or "Because you're having difficulty completing your math when you're seated next to Alberto, *I've decided that* you'll be sitting next to my desk for math."

Notice, *having an expectation* and *imposing a solution* aren't the same thing. In the first example, keeping hands to self when in line walking to recess is the expectation the student is having difficulty meeting; the imposed solution is walking next to the teacher. In the second example, completing the math work is the expectation the student is having difficulty meeting; sitting next to the teacher is the imposed solution. So don't get confused: using Plan A to solve a problem is not the same thing as having an expectation. Put a different way, just because you have an expectation doesn't mean you're using Plan A.

That's important, because one of the common reactions to the CPS model—especially the part of the model that discourages the use of Plan A—is that it involves abandoning all expectations. It doesn't involve anything of the sort. You still have expectations, lots of 'em. How you go about handling *unmet* expectations— unilaterally or collaboratively—is a completely different matter.

There are a few drawbacks with using Plan A to solve problems. The first is that *Plan A greatly heightens the likelihood of challenging behavior in challenging kids.* The vast majority of incompatibility episodes that occur in schools (and everywhere else) are precipitated by an adult responding to a problem (often emergently) using Plan A. Using Plan A might make a great deal of sense if it were your only option for solving problems, but it's not.

The second drawback is that solutions arrived at through Plan A are *uninformed.* Such solutions are based on adult *theories* about the cause of the problem, but not on any information from the intended beneficiary of the solution: the kid. With Plan A, you're not seeking that information. And that's why solutions arrived at through use of Plan A tend not to work very well or for very long.

The third drawback is that Plan A *does not involve the student in solving the problems that affect his life*. Why would we want to exclude students from participating in solving the problems that affect their lives? Isn't the ability to solve problems going to be a crucial skill for doing well in The Real World?

Fourth, Plan A does not lend itself to an adult-child problem-solving partnership. In fact, Plan A typically has the effect of pushing kids away. Why would we want to push kids away when we could be working in partnership with them?

Why do the problems that affect kids' lives so often cause conflict between them and their caregivers? Plan A is a big part of the answer. But those problems don't need to cause conflict, especially if there's a non-adversarial way to solve them. And there is.

Can you get away with Plan A with "ordinary" kids? Perhaps. But why would you want to? The drawbacks involved in using Plan A with behaviorally challenging kids are equally applicable to "ordinary" kids, except that ordinary kids are less prone to exhibit severe challenging behavior in response to Plan A. Don't we want to be partnering with well-behaved kids too? We'll consider those questions more thoroughly in chapter 9.

Plan A has historically been a very popular way of solving problems with kids. Perhaps that explains why we're still losing so many of our most vulnerable kids. Why is Plan A still so popular in so many schools? Because we didn't know how to solve problems any other way. But we know now.

PLAN B

Any problem that can be solved using Plan A can also be solved using Plan B. The primary difference between the two Plans is that with Plan A, problems are being solved unilaterally, and with Plan B, problems are being solved collaboratively. But that's a massive difference.

> *Any problem that can be solved using Plan A can also be solved using Plan B.*

Plan B helps adults clarify and understand a child's concern, perspective, or point of view on a particular unsolved problem. Plan B also helps the kid understand the adult's concerns about the problem. And Plan B helps adults and kids work together, as partners, toward mutually satisfactory solutions so that both parties' concerns are addressed, the student is involved in solving the problems that affect his life, the problem gets solved durably, and lagging skills get taught.

There are two ways to use Plan B: *emergently* and *proactively*. On first hearing about Plan B, adults often come to the erroneous conclusion that the best time to use Plan B is at the precise moment when a kid is beginning to show signs of challenging behavior. But that's Emergency Plan B, and the timing is actually not ideal because the kid may already be upset or heated up and because, if you're a teacher, you've got a lot of other things going on in your classroom at that moment. Few of us do our clearest thinking or resolve difficult problems when we're already upset, so crisis management is not your best long-term strategy; crisis prevention is far preferable. Because incompatibility episodes are highly predictable, you don't have to wait until a problem has popped up yet again to start solving it. As you've read, problems don't just pop up. The goal is to solve them before they occur. That's Proactive Plan B. You'll learn about the three steps of Plan B in the next chapter.

See a teacher engage in basic, Proactive Plan B with his student Charlie. Go to http://livesinthebalance.org/step-three-third-video.

PLAN C

Plan C involves setting aside a given unsolved problem, at least temporarily. As you've read, Plan C is crucial to the process of prioritizing. Recall that behaviorally challenging students usually have quite a few unsolved problems, and that it won't be possible to solve them all at once. Some unsolved problems will need to be set aside for now so that both the student and his caregivers are more "available" to work on higher-priority problems. Expectations that have been removed won't cause incompatibility episodes because they've been eliminated for now.

There are also *emergent* and *proactive* forms of Plan C. The latter form is again preferable. If you've already used the ALSUP to identify the wide array of unsolved problems that are causing incompatibility episodes, and if you've already decided on high and low priorities, then you're well positioned to use Proactive Plan C.

Here's what that might sound like: "Max, you know how we're working on helping you get caught up on that English project you fell behind on? And we're also trying to work on the difficulties you're having getting to school on time. And we've also been trying to find a way to get you caught up on your science lab reports. We're working on a lot of things right now. Should we hold off on working on the geography report that was due a few weeks ago until we get some of these other problems solved?"

And here's what Emergency Plan C sounds like:

TEACHER, WITH AN EXPECTATION: *Class, it's time to get to work on your social studies projects.*
STUDENT: *I'm not doing my social studies project.*
TEACHER, USING PLAN C: *OK.*

OK forever? No, OK for now. The classroom teacher can get the rest of the class started on the social studies project and then check in with this student to gather information about his (apparently) sudden refusal to work on the project. Then the teacher can decide whether this problem is a high priority right now; if it is, the teacher would handle the problem (proactively) with Plan B. If it's not, the teacher would set the problem aside for now, perhaps by proactively discussing with the student how best to do that. But because this probably isn't the first sign of trouble on the social studies project, a more proactive approach was probably possible in the first place.

Does this mean you're supposed to drop all your expectations so a kid won't have incompatibility episodes? No, it doesn't mean that at all. But, again, it is very productive to set aside lower-priority expectations so that you and the student aren't overwhelmed trying to solve too many problems at once.

Q & A

Question: I'm a classroom teacher, and I really do feel that Plan B is best left to the psychologists.

Answer: You may be selling yourself short. If you work in a school, you solve problems with students all the time. Now we're just formalizing the process a little and making it collaborative and proactive. So helping kids solve the problems that affect their lives isn't, and shouldn't be, solely the responsibility of mental health professionals. Because it's collaborative, you're going to be an essential participant in the process anyway.

Question: Aren't there some things a student just has to do?

Answer: There certainly are expectations you feel very strongly that a student should meet. And many caregivers believe that Plan A is the clear choice if they feel really strongly about a student meeting a particular expectation. But it's not. The importance of an expectation is not the determining factor in using Plan A or Plan B. The decisive factor is whether the problem will be best and most durably solved unilaterally or collaboratively. Consideration of whether prior applications of Plan A have solved the problem will help point you in the right direction.

Question: Are there some challenging kids who are so volatile and unstable that academics need to be de-emphasized until things are calmer?

Answer: Absolutely. Some kids simply aren't "available" for academic learning until headway has been made on the nonacademic challenges that may be impeding learning. In such instances, academics may have to take a backseat until progress occurs on these challenges. Plunging forward with academics when a kid is bogged down with other challenges is usually an exercise in futility.

Question: So, just making sure I'm clear here: simply having and voicing an expectation is not the same thing as Plan A, right?

Answer: Right. This is a common point of confusion. Simply voicing an expectation—for example, *"Class, it's time to come in from recess"*—is not Plan A. If you impose a solution to an expectation a student is having difficulty meeting—for example, *"Matt, because you're having difficulty coming back into the classroom for recess, I've decided you're not going out for recess anymore"*—that's Plan A.

Question: So if my expectation is being met, I don't need a Plan?

Answer: Right. You only need the Plans for unmet expectations.

Question: Does Plan B hold kids accountable for their actions?

Answer: For many caregivers, holding a kid accountable for his actions simply means making sure he pays the price for his challenging behavior. That's an extremely narrow definition. If a kid is participating in Plan B, identifying and articulating his concerns, taking yours into account, and working toward a realistic and mutually satisfactory solution, he's most assuredly being held accountable. The belief that Plan A is the only way to hold a kid accountable is completely misguided.

> *The belief that Plan A is the only way to hold a kid accountable is completely misguided.*

Question: Should I still be using consequences for challenging behavior—even if I don't think they're working—so that the other kids know I'm taking the challenging behavior seriously?

Answer: The other kids don't need you to use consequences to know you're taking the problem seriously. They need to see that you've got a handle on the challenging kid's lagging skills and unsolved problems and that, slowly but surely, his incompatibility episodes are decreasing in frequency, intensity, and duration. *You don't improve your credibility by continuing to intervene in a way that isn't working or is making things worse.* Remember, consequences are useful for two things: (1) teaching basic lessons about right and wrong, and (2) giving kids the incentive to do well. You'll want to use consequences if you think one or both of these things are coming into play. But kids with behavioral challenges already know the basic lessons about right and wrong, and—because *kids do well if they can*—they already have the incentive to do well.

Question: Should I reward a kid for successfully participating in Plan B?

Answer: I generally recommend against it. The effects of Plan B—finally having one's concerns heard and identified, making headway on getting problems solved, learning new skills, resolving difficulties without conflict or challenging behavior—are far more rewarding (and far more important for you and the kid to focus on) than any extrinsic reward you might offer.

Question: So I guess I don't need my sticker chart anymore.

Answer: Perhaps not.

EXPERIENCE IS THE BEST TEACHER

" When we first started working on CPS in our building, people were feeling that our school was out of control. Staff members felt like we really needed more support with our most challenging students. And the bottom line was that we weren't going to get more support. We had to do it on our own." "

—NINA, PRINCIPAL

"We had to move away from the idea that it's the parents' responsibility to handle problems that are occurring at school. We shifted to, 'OK, now we're going to be solving problems with the kids and collaborating.' It became clear that we—the people working with the kid at school—were the ones best positioned to help make changes in kids' lives at school." "

—KATHY, TEACHER

"I think that it really all comes down to one thing—curiosity. Don't get frustrated about the kid's behavior, get *curious* about the problem causing the behavior. A lot of adults want the problem to be fixed and better immediately, and I think a lot of adults are used to a model of communication where they lead, and the student does what they say, and then they get results. And Plan B reverses that paradigm. In this way, there's a lot of overlap between current practices in classroom instruction and the philosophy of CPS. They're very closely related, and I think that that's a big shift. Those teachers who struggle the most with best practice in classroom instruction also struggle with what I would consider to be best practice in managing behavior . . . which is to solve problems collaboratively and proactively." "

—TOM, ASSISTANT SUPERINTENDENT

"Proactive Plan B is definitely preferable, especially when you are just starting to have discussions with a student. It's a lot easier to build a relationship that's built on trust and empathy when you're not in the heat of the moment." "

—KATHY, TEACHER

"I remember after many Plan B discussions, teachers would say, 'I had no idea that's what was going on for that student. I never would have guessed that in a million years.' " "

—CAROL, PRINCIPAL

"It's not about doing something more that takes more time. It's using your time doing something different, because you can be using the same ineffective strategy time and time again, and you're spending a lot of time, but you're not making any progress. But if you invest that time in a model that actually can show some progress—and the time that you're expending is getting you somewhere—you're not just spinning your wheels. So I don't think it's about trying to find time; it's just making your time mean something more.**

—NINA, PRINCIPAL

As a school moves in this direction, it's important to let teachers know—and reassure them—that you're not throwing the baby out with the bathwater. There are still going to be basic expectations and rules and procedures in your school for maintaining order. But you're primarily starting with those children for whom you can clearly see that the old system is not working. So reassure teachers that they're not being asked to completely give up some things in order to try something that's going to take a while to put in place and master.

—CAROL, PRINCIPAL

All of us know what the children need, and solving problems with kids and seeing them grow is what feeds us as well. That's the rewarding part of the job.

—NINA, PRINCIPAL

We have to keep our practices child centered. We have to keep asking, 'What are the best practices for the kids in our school?'

—CAROL, PRINCIPAL

Having worked in education for over twenty-three years, I have used Plan A, Plan B, and Plan C at different times and with students in all grade levels, K–12. There is no question that, in my experience, Plan B is the most durable, lasting way to support students in successfully solving the problems that school can present for them. Other strategies are 'quick fixes' and may last for a short time, but as educators, if we really want to help our students in the most meaningful way, our time is best spent using Plan B.

—RYAN, ASSISTANT PRINCIPAL

CHAPTER 6

THE HOW TO

There are three steps involved in solving a problem collaboratively: the Empathy step, the Define Adult Concerns step, and the Invitation step. In this chapter, you'll be reading quite a bit about each step. Even though you may already be familiar with the three steps, you'll probably find information in this chapter that takes you even further.

THE EMPATHY STEP: GATHERING INFORMATION AND UNDERSTANDING

The Empathy step is where you'll be gathering information from a student about her concern, perspective, or point of view on a specific expectation she's having difficulty meeting. You'll be doing that proactively most of the time.

Just like adults, kids have important, legitimate concerns: fatigue, fear, a preference for doing (and not doing) certain things, and the tendency to avoid things that are scary or that make them

75

uncomfortable or at which they don't feel competent. Your mission in the Empathy step is to demonstrate to the student that you're really interested in and curious about those concerns.

How do you do that? When you're using Proactive Plan B, the process of information gathering and understanding begins with an introduction to the unsolved problem. The introduction usually begins with the words *"I've noticed that . . ."* and ends with the words *"What's up?"* In between, you're inserting an unsolved problem. The introduction is made much easier—and, as you know, the likelihood that the student will respond is much greater—if you stick with the general guidelines for writing unsolved problems you read about in chapter 4. Here are some examples of what the introduction would sound like, using some unsolved problems from prior chapters:

"I've noticed that you're having difficulty moving from English to social studies. What's up?"
"I've noticed that you're having difficulty moving from recess back into the classroom. What's up?"
"I've noticed that you're having difficulty completing the word problems on the worksheet in math. What's up?"
"I've noticed that you're having difficulty getting started on the geography project in history. What's up?"

Pretty straightforward so far, yes? Before we get to the hard parts, let's review a few points. First, you're not teaching any lessons in the Empathy step. Actually, you're not teaching lessons in *any* of the three steps. You're not being judgmental either. You're also not saying many of the standard things adults say in response to kids' concerns. So you wouldn't respond to *"I don't like sitting next to Alberto"* with *"Oh, come on, he's not so bad!"* You wouldn't respond to *"The double-digit division problems are too hard for me"* with *"Oh, you'll be fine . . . we just need some more effort here."* And you wouldn't respond to *"I don't want to work with Tina on the Galileo project"* with *"Part of growing up is learning to work with people we don't like."* These are responses that cause kids to feel (often accurately) that their concerns are being ignored, disregarded, dismissed, diminished, or blown off the table. They also cause kids to stop talking. Then you don't have a problem-solving partner, and the problems don't get solved.

> *We adults often think we already know what's getting in the kid's way on a given problem, which may help explain why we often don't put much energy into finding out.*

Some adults have never considered it especially important to gather information about and understand a kid's concern, perspective, or point of view. That's why many kids—perhaps most, unfortunately—are accustomed to having their concerns go unheeded and unaddressed. After all, we adults often think we *already know* what's getting in the kid's way on a given problem, which may help explain why we often don't put much energy into finding out. As you've read, the bad news is that, quite often, our assumptions about kids' concerns are way off base. That's why our solutions—which are based on those assumptions—often turn out to be ineffective. Still more bad news: kids who are accustomed to having their concerns dismissed tend to be far less receptive to hearing *your* concerns. The Empathy step doesn't require that you be a skilled mind reader, but you do need to become highly skilled at gathering information from your students.

Another reason adults tend to blow past kids' concerns is that we have concerns of our own, which we're eager to express. And often we've already decided on a solution anyway, one that addresses only our own concerns and that we're busy imposing.

Those are habits that we'll need to break.

Now on to the hard parts. After you ask, *"What's up?"* one of five things is going to happen:

Possibility 1: She says something.
Possibility 2: She says nothing or *"I don't know."*

Possibility 3: She says, *"I don't have a problem with that."*

Possibility 4: She says, *"I don't want to talk about it right now."*

Possibility 5: She becomes defensive and says something like, *"I don't have to talk to you"* (or worse).

Let's flesh out each of these possibilities.

Possibility 1: She Says Something

If, after the problem is introduced, the student starts talking, that's good. Now you need to keep her talking, because her initial response is unlikely to provide you with a clear understanding of her concern, perspective, or point of view. You're going to need to probe for more information. The probing process—called "drilling for information"—is actually pretty hard for many adults, especially in the beginning, mostly because they're not sure what to say. Difficulty with drilling causes many Plan B ships to run aground, thereby causing many Plan B captains to abandon ship. The good news is that there are some strategies to help you master the drilling process so that the Plan B boat stays afloat.

First, notice, the word is "drill," not "grill." The primary goal of drilling is to *clarify,* whereas grilling tends to be an act of intimidation, or a sign that you anticipate that the student won't be forthcoming or will lie. Your goal is to demonstrate to the student that your attempt to understand her concern or perspective isn't fake or perfunctory. You're really curious . . . *you really want to understand.*

Second, *drilling* is not the same thing as *talking.* There are educators who frequently talk to their students, but never achieve a clear understanding of students' concerns or perspectives on specific unsolved problems. Drilling is much harder than simply talking.

The following drilling strategies should help in the Knowing What to Say Department:

Drilling Strategy 1—Use Reflective listening

This is where you're simply mirroring or repeating back whatever the student just said to you. Let's say you inquired about a student having difficulty sitting next to her classmate, Alberto, during circle time. If the student responds with, "I just don't like it," your response would be, *"Ah, you just don't like it."* Then you'd add a clarifying question or statement, such as *"How so?"* or *"I don't quite understand"* or *"I'm confused"* or *"Can you say more about that?"* or *"What do you mean?"* If this sounds a little basic, maybe so. But reflective listening is your default drilling strategy. It helps kids feel heard. It helps kids feel understood. It clarifies and validates their concerns. And it keeps them talking. You could ask for nothing more from a drilling strategy. If you're in the midst of the Empathy step and you're not sure what to say or which drilling strategy to use, reflective listening is always a safe bet.

> *Reflective listening is your default drilling strategy. It helps kids feel heard. It helps kids feel understood. It clarifies and validates their concerns. And it keeps them talking.*

Drilling Strategy 2—Ask "W questions" (*who, what,* or *where/ when*)

These questions are another good way to demonstrate that you're really listening and need additional information. Examples: *"Who's been giving you a hard time on the school bus?"* *"What's making it hard for you to complete your science homework?"* *"Where/ when is Kyle teasing you?"* Remember, drilling is about gathering information, and "W questions" are a straightforward way to do so. Notice that there's another W question—*Why?*—that you should not be asking very often; that question often elicits the kid's *theory,* and quite possibly one that the child inherited from an adult.

Drilling Strategy 3—Ask about the situational nature of the unsolved problem

At times, it may appear as though the student is actually capable of meeting a given expectation because she sometimes does. This often leads adults to jump to the conclusion that the kid can meet the expectation *when she feels like it*, and that she doesn't meet the expectation when she *doesn't* feel like it. The reality is that there may be nuanced, subtle differences between similar expectations that explain the inconsistency. Rather than jump to conclusions related to poor motivation—"*I know she can do the math when she wants to! She did it yesterday!*"— you'd be better off seeking clarification from the student. Remember, when you're drilling, you're off the hook for mind reading or figuring things out on your own. Here's what this strategy might sound like: "*So, help me understand how you're able to do the math homework sometimes and sometimes you can't.*" Or "*So, sometimes you're on time for school and other times you're not. Help me understand that.*"

Drilling Strategy 4—Ask the student what she's *thinking* in the midst of the unsolved problem

This is an outstanding drilling strategy. "*So, when you're sitting at your desk trying to do the double-digit division problems, what are you thinking?*" Notice, you're not asking her what she's *feeling*. It's not that asking a student what she's feeling is a crime; it's just that the answer (happy, sad, frustrated, embarrassed, bored) won't generally provide you with the information you're seeking about her concern, perspective, or point of view. Also notice that you're not asking her what she *needs* . . . that question is more likely to prompt her to offer a *solution* rather than a *concern*, and you're not ready to start thinking about solutions until the Invitation step.

Drilling Strategy 5—Break the unsolved problem down into its component parts

Most unsolved problems have multiple components. For example, coming into the classroom to get started with the school day has different components (hang up your coat, take off your snow boots, sit down at your desk, start your morning reading assignment, and so on). And getting ready to go home at the end of the day has components (reviewing homework assignments, packing up your backpack with the necessary materials for homework, putting on snow boots and coat, going to the school bus, and so on). But kids sometimes need help identifying those components so that they can tell which component is causing them to struggle:

TEACHER, INTRODUCTION: *I've noticed that it's been difficult for you to get ready to go home at the end of the school day. What's up?*

STUDENT: *I don't know.*

TEACHER: *Do you want to think about it a little?*

STUDENT, AFTER THINKING: *I really don't know.*

TEACHER: *Would it help if we thought about the different parts of getting ready to go home at the end of the school day?*

STUDENT: *OK.*

TEACHER: *Well, first you have to look at your homework sheet so you can figure out what materials you're going to need for homework that night. Is that hard?*

STUDENT: *No.*

TEACHER: *So you're not having any difficulty looking at your homework sheet so you can figure out what materials you're going to need for homework that night?*

STUDENT: *No.*

TEACHER: *OK, the next thing you need to do is get all the materials you're going to need into your backpack. Is that part hard?*

STUDENT: *Getting things into my backpack?*

TEACHER: *Yes.*

STUDENT: *Yes.*

TEACHER: *It is? What's hard about it?*

STUDENT: *I can't always find everything I'm going to need.*

TEACHER: *What's hard about finding everything you need?*

STUDENT: *Sometimes I work with Mrs. Cassidy in a different room, and sometimes I leave stuff in her room. And sometimes I'm not sure if the stuff I need is in my locker, because I might have left it somewhere else. And sometimes Tim asks if he can borrow my books, and sometimes he doesn't give stuff back.*

TEACHER: *I think I understand.*

Good. That's better than not understanding.

> Watch an administrator practice drilling strategies with a student having trouble in some of her classes. Go to http://livesinthebalance.org/step-three-fourth-video.

Drilling Strategy 6—Make a discrepant observation

This involves making an observation that differs from what the student has described about a particular situation. It's the riskiest (in terms of causing the child to stop talking) of all the drilling strategies. That's because many kids—perhaps especially those frequently accused of lying—misinterpret a discrepant observation as an accusation of dishonesty. Fortunately, you're not accusing her of lying; you're simply pointing out that your observations differ from hers. Just because your experience of reality differs from the student's doesn't mean she's lying. She's entitled to her reality.

Here's what a discrepant observation might sound like: *"I know you're saying that you and Felicia are getting along fine these days, but yesterday at recess you two weren't getting along very well at all. What do you think was going on with that?"*

Drilling Strategy 7—Table (and ask for more concerns)

This is where you're "shelving" some concerns the child has already articulated so as to facilitate consideration of other concerns. You're not dismissing the earlier concerns; you're just putting them on the back burner temporarily so as to clear space for consideration of other possible concerns.

Example: *"So if you didn't leave things in Mrs. Cassidy's room, and if you knew whether the things you need for homework were in your locker, and if Tim was giving you back the things he borrowed . . . would there be anything else that would make it difficult for you get ready to go home at the end of the day?"*

Drilling Strategy 8—Summarize (and ask for more concerns)

This is where you're summarizing concerns you've already heard about and then asking if there are any other concerns that haven't yet been discussed. This is the recommended strategy to use before moving on to the Define Adult Concerns step, just to make sure there are no other concerns.

Example: *"Let me make sure I understand everything you've said. It's hard for you to ride on the school bus because it's too loud, and because they're making you sit three to a seat so it's really crowded, and because you never get to sit on the aisle, and because Steve is picking on you and the bus driver always blames you. Is there anything else that's hard for you about riding on the school bus?"*

By the way, these eight strategies are summarized on the Drilling Cheat Sheet. In your first twenty Plan Bs, you may want to have it in front of you for easy reference.

DRILLING CHEAT SHEET

The goal of the Empathy step is to gather information from the child about his or her concern or perspective on the unsolved problem you're discussing (preferably proactively). For many adults, this is the most difficult part of Plan B, as they often find that they are at a loss for words and unsure of what to ask next. So here's a brief summary of different strategies for drilling for information:

Reflective Listening and Clarifying Statements

Reflective listening basically involves repeating what a child has said and then encouraging her to provide additional information by using clarifying questions or statements.

Examples of Clarifying Questions and Statements:

- *"How so?"*
- *"I don't quite understand."*
- *"I'm confused."*
- *"Can you say more about that?"*
- *"What do you mean?"*

Reflective listening is your "default" drilling strategy. If you aren't sure of which strategy to use or what to say next, use this strategy.

Asking About the Who, What, Where/When of the Unsolved Problem

Examples:

- *"Who was making fun of your clothes?"*
- *"What's getting in the way of completing the science project?"*
- *"Where is Eddie bossing you around?"*

Asking about Why the Problem Occurs under Some Conditions and Not Others

Example:

"You seem to be doing really well with Taylor in your work group in math . . . but not so well in your work group in social studies . . . what's getting in the way in social studies?"

Asking the Child What She's *Thinking* in the Midst of the Unsolved Problem

Notice, this is different than asking the child what she is *feeling*, which doesn't usually provide much information about the child's concern or perspective on an unsolved problem.

Example:

"What were you thinking when Mrs. Thompson told the class to get to work on the science quiz?"

Breaking the Problem Down into Its Component Parts

Example:

"So writing the answers to the questions on the science quiz is hard for you . . . but you're not sure why. Let's think about the different parts of answering questions on the science quiz. First, you have to understand what the question is asking. Is that part hard for you? Next, you need to think of the answer to the question. Is that part hard? Next, you have to remember the answer long enough to write it down. Are you having trouble with that part? Then you have to actually do the writing. Any trouble with that part?"

Making a Discrepant Observation

This involves making an observation that differs from what the child is describing about a particular situation. It's the riskiest (in terms of causing the child to stop talking) of all the drilling strategies.

Example:

"I know you're saying that you haven't been having any difficulty with Chad on the playground lately, but I recall a few times last week when you guys were having a big disagreement about the rules in the four-square game. What do you think was going on with that?"

Tabling (and Asking for More Concerns)

This is where you're "shelving" some concerns the child has already discussed so as to permit consideration of other concerns.

Example:

"So if Timmy wasn't sitting too close to you, and Robbie wasn't making noises, and the floor wasn't dirty, and the buttons in your pants weren't bothering you . . . is there anything else that would make it difficult for you to participate in Morning Meeting?"

Summarizing (and Asking for More Concerns)

This is where you're summarizing concerns you've already heard about and then asking if there are any other concerns that haven't yet been discussed. This is the recommended strategy to use before moving on to the Define Adult Concerns step.

Example:

"Let me make sure I understand all of this correctly. It's hard for you to do your social studies worksheet for homework because writing down the answers is still hard for you, and because sometimes you don't understand the question, and because Mrs. Langley hasn't yet covered the material on the worksheet. Is there anything else that's hard for you about completing the social studies worksheet for homework?"

To download the Drilling Cheat Sheet, go to www.livesinthebalance.org/LostandFound.

Here's an example of what drilling might sound like, with examples of some of the different drilling strategies, with a younger student:

TEACHER: *I've noticed that you've been having difficulty keeping your hands to yourself standing in line on the way to lunch. What's up?*

LARA: *It's not fair.*

TEACHER, USING REFLECTIVE LISTENING: *It's not fair. I'm sorry; I don't quite understand what you mean. What's not fair?*

LARA: *It's not fair how you do the lines.*

TEACHER, USING REFLECTIVE LISTENING AGAIN: *It's not fair how I do the lines. I'm still a little confused. Can you help me understand what you mean?*

LARA: *You always make me walk with you in the back of the line.*

TEACHER, ASKING A W QUESTION: *Well, yes, I've been having you walk with me in the back of the line for the past week or so because you've been having trouble keeping your hands to yourself. But now I'm trying to understand what's making it hard for you to keep your hands to yourself. Can you help me understand that better?*

LARA: *(shrugs)*

TEACHER, REPEATING THE W QUESTION: *Well, think about it for a minute. We're not in a rush. What's making it hard for you to keep your hands to yourself when you're in line on the way to lunch?*

LARA: *I want to be in front of Emily.*

TEACHER, USING REFLECTIVE LISTENING: *You want to be in front of Emily. Help me understand that.*

LARA: *Emily's always in front of me because of the way you do the lines.*

TEACHER, USING A W QUESTION: *What is it about having Emily in front of you that you don't like?*

LARA: *I never get to be first in line.*

TEACHER, USING REFLECTIVE LISTENING: *You never get to be first in line. What do you mean?*

LARA: *I've never been first in line.*

TEACHER: *You haven't?*

LARA: *Never.*

TEACHER: *Because we go in alphabetical order, and you're right after Emily. You haven't had your turn at being first in line?*

LARA: *You skipped me.*

TEACHER: *I did?*

LARA: *You had Emily be first in line twice. Then we went to the back of the line again. I got skipped.*

TEACHER: *Lara, I didn't know that. How come you didn't say anything?*

LARA: *I tried. You told me to be quiet.*

TEACHER: *I'm sorry, Lara. I don't remember you trying to tell me that, but it's definitely something I would have wanted to know. I'm glad you told me now.*

LARA: *(nods)*

TEACHER, SUMMARIZING: *So one of the reasons you're having difficulty keeping your hands to yourself when you're standing in line for lunch is that you want to be in front of Emily because she got to be first in line and you didn't. Are there any other reasons?*

LARA: *Kenny keeps stepping on the back of my shoe.*

TEACHER, USING REFLECTIVE LISTENING: *Kenny keeps stepping on the back of your shoe. Is he behind you in line?*

LARA: *Uh-huh. He thinks it's funny when my shoe comes off. So I try to keep him from being too close to me.*

TEACHER: *And how do you do that?*

LARA: *I push him.*

TEACHER, SUMMARIZING AGAIN: *Goodness, I'm learning a lot here. So one of the reasons you have trouble keeping your hands to yourself is that Kenny is stepping on the back of your shoe. And another reason is that you want to be first in line because we skipped your turn.*

LARA: *(nodding)*

TEACHER: *Any other reasons?*

LARA: *That's it.*

TEACHER: *You sure?*

LARA: *Uh-huh.*

OK, so you didn't see every drilling strategy there, but you saw a lot of them. Don't worry, examples of Plan B with older, less congenial students are coming up soon. And the next two steps of Plan B on this problem are coming up soon too. In the meantime, let's think about what was accomplished in that Empathy step. First, the teacher had a fairly standard experience: she obtained new information that differed from her original theory (Lara comes from a tough neighborhood where shoving people is the norm). She also learned why her stopgap solution (having Lara stand in the back of the line with her) won't solve the problem durably: the solution doesn't address Lara's concerns. Because she's solving this problem collaboratively—in partnership with Lara—the teacher has increased the likelihood that Lara will partner with her in solving other problems. And maybe, just maybe, the solution to this problem will be applicable to other circumstances in which Lara is having similar problems keeping her hands to herself when she's standing in line. Nice work.

> *No matter how fast or slow the Empathy step, you're still saving time. That's because solved problems always take a lot less time than unsolved problems.*

By the way, that was a quick Empathy step. Many early Empathy steps—with kids who have many concerns but haven't been provided a forum for expressing them—may last up to thirty minutes. Later Empathy steps tend to be faster. But no matter how fast or slow the Empathy step, you're still saving time. Again, that's because solved problems always take a lot less time than unsolved problems.

Possibility 2: She Says Nothing or "I Don't Know"

This is another possible way in which a student might respond to your initial introduction to an unsolved problem. There are lots of reasons a kid might say nothing or "I don't know."

Your wording is off.

If you don't word unsolved problems according to the guidelines in chapter 4, you'll increase the likelihood of silence or *"I don't know,"* often because the kid doesn't completely understand what you're inquiring about or believes that she's in trouble or that you're mad. Perhaps you've only been talking with her about problems when you *are* mad or she *is* in trouble, so you'll want to reassure her that you're actually just trying to understand her concerns and solve the problem together.

Your timing is off.

Remember, Emergency Plan B adds heat and time pressure to the mix. Doing Plan B proactively so that the student isn't surprised by your desire to have a discussion—and giving her some advance notice of the topic—can reduce the likelihood of *"I don't know"* and silence as well.

She really doesn't know what her concern is about the problem you're trying to discuss.

Perhaps you've never inquired about her concerns before, at least not in this way. Perhaps she's never given the matter any thought. Perhaps she's become so accustomed to having her concerns dismissed that she hasn't given thought to her concerns for a very long time.

She's had a lot of Plan A in her life, and she's still betting on the Plan A horse.

You'll have to prove to her—by solving problems collaboratively rather than unilaterally—that you're not riding that horse anymore. By the way, mere reassurance about that won't get the job done . . . the proof's in the pudding.

She may be reluctant to say what's on her mind.

Perhaps history has taught her that if she says what she thinks, you'll simply disagree or take offense, and it'll cause conflict. Perhaps your reaction to the problem is at the root of her concern, and she's reluctant to say that. Your goal in the Empathy step is to suspend your emotional response to what the student is saying, knowing that if you react emotionally to what you're hearing, she'll clam up, and you won't end up hearing anything. You badly want to understand her concerns, even if her concerns involve you. If you don't know what her concerns are, those concerns won't get addressed, and the problem will remain unsolved. And she'll remain convinced that you're not listening.

She's buying time.

Many kids say *"I don't know"* instead of *"Umm"* or *"Give me a second"* or *"Let me think about that a minute."* Since you're not in a rush, you'll be able to give her a second and let her think about it a minute. Many kids say nothing because they're collecting their thoughts or because they're having difficulty putting their thoughts into words. Unfortunately, adults often respond to silence by filling the void with their own concerns, theories, or solutions. In such instances, you've strayed quite far from the main goals of the Empathy step (information gathering and understanding) and made it even more difficult for the student to think. You may need to grow more comfortable with the silence that can occur as a kid is giving thought to her concerns.

> *Your goal in the Empathy step is to suspend your emotional response to what the student is saying. . . . If you react emotionally to what you're hearing, she'll clam up, and you won't end up hearing anything.*

If you've given a student the chance to think and it's clear that she really has no idea what her concerns are or is simply unable to put her thoughts into words, your best option is to do some *educated guessing* or *hypothesis testing.* Here, finally, your theories may actually come in handy. Suggest a few possibilities, based on experience, and see if any ring true:

TEACHER: *I've noticed that you've had some difficulty going to recess lately. What's up?*

STUDENT: *I don't know.*

TEACHER: *Well, let's think about it. There's no rush.*

STUDENT, *AFTER FIFTEEN SECONDS: I really don't know.*

TEACHER: *Take your time.*

STUDENT, *AFTER ANOTHER FIVE SECONDS: I really don't know.*

TEACHER: *Hmmm. Well, I know some things you've told me before when you didn't want to go to recess. Do you remember what those things were?*

STUDENT. *No.*

TEACHER: *Well, sometimes you're worried that the other kids will get mad at you if you mess up in the game. Is that it?*

STUDENT: *Kind of. There's some sports I'm not that good at.*

TEACHER: *Which ones?*

STUDENT: *Um . . . like basketball. And four square. But I'm pretty good in kick-ball.*

TEACHER: *What's hard about the other kids getting mad at you?*

STUDENT: *They take it too seriously. Takes the fun out of it.*

TEACHER: *So you said that was kind of the problem. Is there something I'm not understanding about that?*

STUDENT: *No, that's it.*

TEACHER: *Something else you've said is that when there's no organized game going on, you sometimes have trouble finding someone to play with. Is that still true?*

STUDENT: *Not so much. I've been hanging out with Omar and Katie.*

TEACHER: *So it's mainly that you're worried about the kids getting mad at you if you make a mistake?*

STUDENT: *I guess.*

TEACHER: *Well, let's keep thinking . . . maybe there's something else.*

STUDENT: *Um, when kids are being mean to each other, you're not out there, and the recess monitors don't pay attention.*

TEACHER: *No, I'm not out there during recess. Tell me more about the recess monitors.*

STUDENT: *They don't care if kids are mean to each other, even if I tell them.*

TEACHER: *What do they do if you tell them?*

STUDENT: *They just say stuff like, "Work it out."*

TEACHER: *And that doesn't help.*

STUDENT: *No.*

TEACHER: *And are you one of the kids who other kids are mean to a lot?*

STUDENT: *Kind of. But there's other kids too.*

TEACHER: *And what are the kids who are being mean doing that's mean?*

STUDENT: *Um . . . calling names . . . and ruining people games . . . and sometimes stealing the ball . . . stuff like that.*

TEACHER: *Well, I'm very glad you're telling me these things.*

STUDENT: *But I don't want the kids who are being mean knowing that I'm the one who told you.*

TEACHER: *No, this is just between you and me. But I do think I'm going to need some more details. Can we talk about it again tomorrow? I really want to make sure these problems get solved, now that I know about them.*

STUDENT: *What can you do?*

TEACHER: *I'm not sure, but I'd like to see if we can solve them so you can start having fun at recess again.*

Another very nice haul of information, though there are still some concerns that require further clarification. But the student's concerns are now one step closer to getting addressed . . . and the problem is now one step closer to getting solved.

As you're in the midst of hypothesizing, bear in mind that you're proposing *possibilities* rather than divining the kid's concern. Here's what divining sounds like (this is an example of what *not* to do):

TEACHER: *I've noticed that you haven't been too enthusiastic about going to recess lately. What's up?*

KID: *I don't know.*

TEACHER: *I think it's because the weather's getting colder, and you don't like going outside when it's cold. I think you're just going to have to dress warmer.*

Possibility 3: She Says, "I Don't Have a Problem with That"

Many adults think that if a kid says, *"I don't have a problem with that,"* the game is over. After all, how can they talk with the kid about a problem if the kid doesn't have a problem with the problem? But this response isn't a dead end at all; indeed, it's usually the jumping-off point for learning more about her concern, perspective, or point of view. While it's entirely possible that she isn't as concerned about the problem as you are, that doesn't mean you can't proceed with Plan B. The first drilling strategy (reflective listening) should serve you well as an initial response. Here's what it would sound like with an older, more reluctant participant:

TEACHER: *I've noticed it's been difficult for you to get to school lately. What's up?*

STUDENT: *I don't have a problem with that.*

TEACHER: *Ah, you don't have a problem with that. I'm sorry, I'm not sure I understand what you mean.*

STUDENT: *I mean I don't really care if I come to school.*

TEACHER: *Ah, you don't really care if you come to school. Can you say more about that?*

STUDENT: *It doesn't really matter.*

TEACHER: *It doesn't really matter. What do you mean?*

STUDENT: *I'm dropping out as soon as I can anyway.*

TEACHER: *You're dropping out as soon as you can.*

STUDENT: *So there's not much point in being here.*

TEACHER: *I suppose not. But tell me about dropping out.*

STUDENT: *There's no point.*

TEACHER: *There's no point in staying in school or there's no point in talking about it?*

STUDENT: *Um, both, I guess.*

TEACHER: *OK. Well, we don't have to talk about it, but I sure would like to know what's making it so you're going to drop out as soon as you can.*

STUDENT: *I hate it here. I mean, no offense.*

TEACHER: *No offense taken. I really want to understand.*

STUDENT: *Well, you're not talking me out of it.*

TEACHER: *I wasn't going to try.*

STUDENT: *I've never done good in school. Never. I stopped trying a long time ago.*

TEACHER: *When did you stop trying?*

STUDENT: *Like, third grade.*

TEACHER: *That was a long time ago. What caused you to stop trying in the third grade?*

STUDENT: *Do we have to talk about this?*

TEACHER: *No, we don't have to. But I would like to understand.*

STUDENT: *I was getting in trouble a lot . . . and getting suspended a lot . . . and my mom was whupping me every time I got suspended . . . and I couldn't read . . . and they tried helping me with the reading, but it didn't help.*

TEACHER: *So is reading still hard for you?*

STUDENT: *Uh-huh. But I don't want anyone to know.*

TEACHER: *Your secret is safe with me.*

She talked. And it sounds like she has some concerns that have gone unaddressed for a long time. We'll have to learn more about them. Don't worry, we'll come back to that one later in the chapter, too.

Possibility 4: She Says "I Don't Want to Talk About It Right Now"

Fortunately, she doesn't have to talk about it right now, and it's a good idea to let her know that. Many kids start talking the instant they're given permission *not* to talk. If she truly doesn't want to talk about it right now, it's likely she has a good reason; maybe she'll talk about *that*. A lot of kids *will* talk about *why* they don't want to talk about something, which is very informative in its own right. Then, after they're through talking about that, they're comfortable enough to start talking about what they didn't want to talk about in the first place.

TEACHER: *Emily, I've noticed that you had difficulty working with Catherine as your math partner. What's up?*

EMILY: *I don't want to talk about it right now.*

TEACHER: *OK . . . well, you don't have to talk about it right now.*

EMILY: *Or ever.*

TEACHER: *Can you help me understand why you don't want to talk about it?*

EMILY: *Because you'll tell Catherine what I say . . . or you'll make us "work it out" together . . . and I really don't feel like dealing with it. I have too much other stuff going on right now.*

TEACHER: *I'd like to hear about all that you have going on right now. And I'm glad you told me why you don't want to talk about the difficulty with Catherine. I wasn't planning on telling her anything you say—it's just between me and you—and I can't make you work it out with her. So you're safe there, too.*

EMILY: *It's just that she's such a know-it-all . . . and she never lets anyone else talk in class . . . and I can't stand being her math partner . . .*

Good; we seem to be getting somewhere.

> *Many adults respond to a kid's reluctance to talk by insisting harder that the kid talk. But you don't want to try so hard to get the student to talk today that you lose your credibility for tomorrow. There's always tomorrow.*

Regrettably, many adults respond to a kid's reluctance to talk by *insisting harder* that the kid talk. But you don't want to try so hard to get the student to talk today that you lose your credibility for tomorrow. There's always tomorrow. And problem solving is an incremental process.

Possibility 5: She Becomes Defensive and Says Something Like "I Don't Have to Talk to You"

Let's think about why a kid would become defensive in response to adult requests for information on a particular unsolved problem. We've actually covered some of them already. Maybe she's accustomed to having adults impose solutions (Plan A), and her experience is that those solutions haven't addressed her concerns and therefore haven't worked and she doesn't see the point in going down that road anymore. Maybe she thinks that if a problem is being raised, she must be in trouble, so she's anticipating excoriation and punishment. Maybe she doesn't really see the point in contemplating or voicing her concerns because she's become accustomed to having them swept off the table.

Fortunately, we're trying to break the patterns of communication and adult responses that would cause a kid to feel that talking is not her best option. Your best approach to defensive statements is not reciprocal defensiveness or threats of adult-imposed consequences but rather *honesty*. A good response to *"I don't have to talk to you"* would be *"You don't have to talk to me."* A good response to

"You're not my boss" would be *"I'm not trying to boss you."* And a good response to *"You can't make me talk"* would be *"I can't make you talk."* Some reassurance that you're not using Plan A might be helpful, too, as in *"I'm not telling you what to do"* (you're not), *"You're not in trouble"* (she's not), *"I'm not mad at you"* (you're not), and *"I'm just trying to understand"* (you are). Statements like *"I'm doing this [imposing this solution] because it's what's best for you"* would not be ideal.

You're ready to move on to the Define Adult Concerns step when you have a clear understanding of the student's concern or perspective on a given unsolved problem. How do you know when you've reached that point? Keep summarizing and asking for more information (drilling strategy 8) until she has no additional concerns.

THE DEFINE ADULT CONCERNS STEP: YOUR CONCERNS MATTER A LOT, TOO

The student is not the only one with concerns, and often not the only one whose concerns need to be clarified and articulated. You have concerns as well, and you want those concerns to be heard and addressed. Your time has come.

This step is made difficult primarily by the fact that adults often rush past their concerns and start proposing (and often imposing) their *solutions*. But solutions that are proposed before identifying the concerns of both parties won't work, since they can't possibly address those respective concerns. If the student reciprocates with solutions of her own, then you and she are now engaged in an all-too-common state of affairs called a power struggle. Power struggles result when two parties (for example, you and a student, but that's not the only possible combination of players) are proposing *competing solutions* that do not address the concerns of both parties. There's no such thing as *competing concerns*, by the way, only different concerns that need to be addressed. The concerns of one party don't trump the concerns of the other, and the goal isn't to establish whose concerns are "right" and whose are "wrong." The concerns of both parties are of exactly equal legitimacy. That doesn't mean the kid is your equal. But if you want to solve problems collaboratively with her, then her concerns are no less valid and meaningful than yours.

You'll need to give some careful thought to your concerns, and you can do that ahead of time if you're finding it hard to think about them in the moment. Simply restating the *expectation* the student is having difficulty meeting—*"I really want to see more science homework coming in"*—would *not* be an expression of your *concerns*. Rather, your concerns will almost always fall into one or both of two categories:

1. How the unsolved problem is affecting the student
2. How the unsolved problem is affecting others

> *Expressions of adult concerns usually begin with the words "The thing is . . ." or "My concern is ". . ." but most definitely not "That is all well and good, but . . ."*

Expressions of adult concerns usually begin with the words *"The thing is . . ."* or *"My concern is . . ."* but most definitely not *"That is all well and good, but . . ."* Let's see what some typical adult concerns might be for some of the problems we've been discussing. At the end of each example, you'll see which of the two categories the concerns fall into.

Difficulty moving from English to social studies: *"My concern is that if you're late for social studies, you'll miss some of the lesson, and it'll be hard for you to understand what's going on."* (1)

Difficulty completing the word problems on the worksheet in math: *"My concern is that you're missing out on some important practice in math."* (1)

Difficulty getting to school: *"My concern is that if you don't come to school, then there's no way I can help you with the things you've been struggling with . . . and that if you don't get a high school diploma, it's going to make it harder for you to get a job . . . and that when you do come to school, you're way behind in class and sometimes distract your classmates."* (1 and 2)

Difficulty going to recess: *"My concern is that if you don't go to recess, you'll miss out on the fun . . . and that it's good for you to have a break from what we're doing in class."* (1)

Difficulty keeping hands to self in line for lunch: *"My concern is that someone could get hurt, and I want to make sure everyone in our class feels safe, including you."* (2)

You'll see more of the Define Adult Concerns step when we return to some of our earlier dialogues after we cover the Invitation.

THE INVITATION STEP: COLLABORATING ON SOLUTIONS

This final step involves considering potential solutions that will address the concerns of both parties, concerns that have been identified and clarified in the first two steps. It's called the Invitation step because you're actually inviting the student to collaborate on solutions. The Invitation lets the student know that solving the problem is something you're doing *with* her (collaboratively) rather than *to* her (unilaterally). Notice you're not collaborating on coming up with a *consequence*; consequences don't solve problems.

To start this step, you could simply say something like, *"Let's think about how we can solve this problem"* or *"Let's think about how we can work that out."* But to facilitate the consideration of solutions that will address the concerns of both parties, it's usually better to recap the concerns that were identified in the first two steps, usually starting with the words *"I wonder if there's a way . . ."* So, for one of our previous examples, that would sound something like this: *"I wonder if there's a way for us to make sure no one gets hurt in the line for lunch* [that was the teacher's concern] *and also make sure that you're first in line sometimes and that Kenny doesn't step on the back of your shoe* [those were the kid's concerns]."

Then you give the student the first opportunity to propose a solution by asking, *"Do you have any ideas?"* This is not an indication that the burden of solving the problem is placed solely on the student. The burden of solving the problem is placed on the Problem Solving Team (the adult and student). But giving the student the first crack at thinking of a solution is a good strategy for letting her know you're actually interested in her ideas. It also gives her practice at thinking of solutions. Too often adults take on the responsibility of coming up with solutions, thereby depriving kids of the opportunity for practice. Although there is a chance that the student won't be able to think of any solutions, it's actually quite likely that she *can* think of solutions, and even ones that will take your combined concerns into account. There's also a good chance that she has been waiting, perhaps not so patiently, for you to give her the chance.

Many adults enter Plan B with a preordained solution. In other words, they already know where the Plan B plane is landing before it takes off. If you already know where the plane is landing before it takes off, you're not using Plan B; you're using a "clever" form of Plan A. Plan B is not just a clever form of Plan A. Plan B is collaborative. Plan A is unilateral.

> *Many adults enter Plan B with a preordained solution. . . . If you already know where the Plan B plane is landing before it takes off, you're not using Plan B; you're using a "clever" form of Plan A.*

The reality is that there is no flight plan. The Plan B plane will head wherever the crosswinds of your combined concerns take you. But you do have some gauges in the cockpit to help you and your problem-solving partner (the student) know where to land the plane: the solution must be *realistic* (meaning that both parties can actually do what they're agreeing to do) and *mutually satisfactory* (meaning that the solution truly and logically addresses the concerns of both parties). If a solution isn't realistic and mutually satisfactory, alternative solutions should be generated and considered. By the way, the solution "try harder" is never viable.

The realistic part is crucial because Plan B isn't an exercise in wishful thinking. If you can't execute your part of a solution that's under consideration, don't agree to it just to end the conversation. Likewise, if you don't think the student can execute her part of a solution that's under consideration, then try to get her to take a moment to think about whether she can actually do what she's agreeing to do. (*"You sure you can do that? Let's make sure we come up with a solution we can both do."*)

The mutually satisfactory part is crucial, too, and requires that you and the student give conscious, deliberate thought to the concerns that the solution is intended to address. In other words, all proposed solutions are evaluated on the basis of whether they address the concerns identified in the first two steps of Plan B. The mutually satisfactory aspect is a great comfort to adults who fear that in using Plan B, their concerns will go unaddressed and no limits will be set. *You're "setting limits" if your concerns are being addressed. And if a solution is mutually satisfactory, then by definition your concerns have been addressed.* In other words, if you thought that Plan A is the only mechanism by which adults can set limits and help students meet expectations, you were mistaken.

The mutually satisfactory part also helps the kid know that *you're as invested in ensuring that her concerns are addressed as you are in making sure that yours are addressed.* That's how you lose an enemy and gain a problem-solving partner. That's how you move from adversary to teammate, from stopgap solutions to durable ones, and from dealing with one incident after another to solving problems.

Early on, the student may come up with solutions that address *her* concerns but not *yours*. (And you may have a tendency to propose solutions that address your concerns and not hers.) That doesn't mean that she's come up with a bad idea—or that she doesn't care about your concerns or is unable to take them into account—only that she's not yet highly skilled at coming up with solutions that are mutually satisfactory. Simply remind her that the goal is to come up with a solution that works for both of you, perhaps by saying, *"Well, that's an idea, and I know that idea would address your concern, but I don't think it would address my concern. Let's see if we can come up with an idea that will work for both of us."*

One last thing. If multiple concerns are expressed in the Empathy step and the Define Adult Concerns step, there's a pretty strong likelihood that the same solution won't address them all. So before considering solutions, it's often necessary to decide which concerns will be addressed in the current discussion and which will be addressed in a later Plan B.

Many adults, in their eagerness to solve the problem, forget the Invitation step. This means that just as they are at the precipice of actually collaborating on a solution, they impose a solution. Not good. The kid thought you were partnering with her in solving a problem and then you went back to being unilateral and pulled the collaborative rug out from under her. She's likely to have major reservations about participating in the process again the next time.

ALL TOGETHER NOW

Let's see how the three ingredients would go together, assuming that things are going smoothly. Again, forgive the redundancy, but it's helpful to see the process unfold from start to finish.

The Empathy Step

TEACHER: *I've noticed that you've been having difficulty keeping your hands to yourself standing in line on the way to lunch. What's up?*

LARA: *It's not fair.*

TEACHER, USING REFLECTIVE LISTENING: *It's not fair. I'm sorry; I don't quite understand what you mean. What's not fair?*

LARA: *It's not fair how you do the lines.*

TEACHER, USING REFLECTIVE LISTENING AGAIN: *It's not fair how I do the lines. I'm still a little confused. Can you help me understand what you mean?*

LARA: *You always make me walk with you in the back of the line.*

TEACHER, ASKING A W QUESTION: *Well, yes, I've been having you walk with me in the back of the line for the past week or so because you've been having trouble keeping your hands to yourself. But now I'm trying to understand what's making it hard for you to keep your hands to yourself. Can you help me understand that better?*

LARA: *(shrugs)*

TEACHER, REPEATING THE W QUESTION: *Well, think about it for a minute. We're not in a rush. What's making it hard for you to keep your hands to yourself when you're in line on the way to lunch?"*

LARA: *I want to be in front of Emily.*

TEACHER, USING REFLECTIVE LISTENING: *You want to be in front of Emily. Help me understand that.*

LARA: *Emily's always in front of me because of the way you do the lines.*

TEACHER, USING A W QUESTION: *What is it about having Emily in front of you that you don't like?*

LARA: *I never get to be first in line.*

TEACHER, USING REFLECTIVE LISTENING: *You never get to be first in line. What do you mean?*

LARA: *I've never been first in line.*

TEACHER: *You haven't?*

LARA. *Never.*

TEACHER: *Because we go in alphabetical order, and you're right after Emily. You haven't had your turn at being first in line?*

LARA: *You skipped me.*

TEACHER: *I did?*

LARA: *You had Emily be first in line twice. Then we went to the back again. I got skipped.*

TEACHER: *Lara, I didn't know that. How come you didn't say anything?*

LARA: *I tried. You told me to be quiet.*

TEACHER: *I'm sorry, Lara. I don't remember you trying to tell me that, but it's definitely something I would have wanted to know. I'm glad you told me now.*

LARA: *(nods)*

TEACHER, SUMMARIZING: *So one of the reasons you're having difficulty keeping your hands to yourself when you're standing in line for lunch is because you want to be in front of Emily because she got to be first in line and you didn't. Are there any other reasons?*

LARA: *Kenny keeps stepping on the back of my shoe.*

TEACHER, USING REFLECTIVE LISTENING: *Kenny keeps stepping on the back of your shoe. Is he behind you in line?*

LARA: *Uh-huh.*

TEACHER, USING A W QUESTION: *What's causing him to step on the back of your shoe?*

LARA: *I don't know. He thinks it's funny when my shoe comes off. So I try to keep him from being too close to me.*

TEACHER: *And how do you do that?*

LARA: *I push him.*

TEACHER, SUMMARIZING AGAIN: *Goodness, I'm learning a lot here. So one of the reasons you have trouble keeping your hands to yourself is that Kenny is stepping on the back of your shoe. And another reason is that you want to be first in line because we skipped your turn.*

LARA: *(nodding)*

TEACHER: *Any other reasons?*

LARA: *That's it.*

TEACHER: *You sure?*

LARA: *Uh-huh.*

The Define Adult Concerns Step

TEACHER: *The thing is, I'm concerned that if you're trying to solve these problems by pushing people or trying to cut in front of them, someone could get hurt. And I want to make sure that everyone in our classroom feels safe, including you. Does that make sense?*

LARA: *Uh-huh.*

The Invitation Step

TEACHER: *So I wonder if there's a way for us to make sure no one gets hurt in the line for lunch and also make sure that you're first in line sometimes and that Kenny doesn't step on the back of your feet. Do you have any ideas?*

LARA: *You could not skip me.*

TEACHER: *Lara, I think that's a very good idea. In fact, it sounds like we owe you a time to be first in line. So we can make sure you're first in line tomorrow. Would that work for you?*

LARA: *Yes. How do I know you won't skip me again?*

TEACHER: *Well, this may be the first time I've ever skipped someone on being first in line. So I'm pretty good at making sure everyone gets their turns. But if I slip, please tell me again. I promise I'll be listening next time. OK?*

LARA: *OK.*

TEACHER: *And how about that other part . . . the part about Kenny stepping on the back of your shoes? What can we do about that so that everyone is safe?*

LARA: *You could always have him at the back of the line with you.*

TEACHER: *Well, there's an idea. Although I don't think he'd like that idea very much. I know you didn't like that solution, so I'm betting he won't either. And we want to come up with a solution that works for him too. Of course, he's not part of our conversation right now, so it might be hard to come up with a solution that works for him. Do you know what I mean?*

LARA: *Yes.*

TEACHER: *Maybe I should talk to him about this problem tomorrow, see what his concerns are, and then maybe get together with you and him to solve the problem together. What do you think?*

LARA: *OK.*

Are you thinking that our first example of all three steps went rather seamlessly? Yes, it was pretty smooth sailing. It's good to see an initial example of all three steps without major glitches. We'll be getting around to glitches in the next chapter. But let's return now to our reluctant participant to see how that discussion turned out too.

TEACHER: *I've noticed it's been difficult for you to get to school lately. What's up?*

STUDENT: *I don't have a problem with that.*

TEACHER: *Ah, you don't have a problem with that. I'm sorry, I'm not sure I understand what you mean.*

STUDENT: *I mean I don't really care if I come to school.*

TEACHER: *Ah, you don't really care if you come to school. Can you say more about that?*

STUDENT: *It doesn't really matter.*

TEACHER: *It doesn't really matter. What do you mean?*

STUDENT: *I'm dropping out as soon as I can anyway.*

TEACHER: *You're dropping out as soon as you can.*

STUDENT: *So there's not much point in being here.*

TEACHER: *I suppose not. But tell me about dropping out.*

STUDENT: *There's no point.*

TEACHER: *There's no point in staying in school or there's no point in talking about it?*

STUDENT: *Um, both, I guess.*

TEACHER: *OK. Well, we don't have to talk about it, but I sure would like to know what's making it so you're going to drop out as soon as you can.*

STUDENT: *I hate it here. I mean, no offense.*

TEACHER: *No offense taken. I really want to understand.*

STUDENT: *Well, you're not talking me out of it.*

TEACHER: *I wasn't going to try.*

STUDENT: *I've never done good in school. Never. I stopped trying a long time ago.*

TEACHER: *When did you stop trying?*

STUDENT: *Like, third grade.*

TEACHER: *That was a long time ago. What caused you to stop trying in the third grade?*

STUDENT: *Do we have to talk about this?*

TEACHER: *No, we don't have to. But I would like to understand.*

STUDENT: *I was getting in trouble a lot . . . and getting suspended a lot . . . and my mom was whupping me every time I got suspended . . . and I couldn't read . . . and they tried helping me with the reading but it didn't help.*

TEACHER: *So is reading still hard for you?*

STUDENT: *Uh-huh. But I don't want anyone to know.*

TEACHER: *Your secret is safe with me. What were you getting in trouble for in the third grade?*

STUDENT: *I was, like, hyper. I couldn't sit there. And they wanted me to, like, take medicine 'cuz I was hyper. But my mom didn't want me to be on medicine. So they finally convinced her, but the medicine made me really cranky. So she didn't give it to me anymore.*

TEACHER: *And when you say you were hyper, what do you mean?*

STUDENT: *Couldn't sit still . . . had to walk around . . . couldn't do my work . . . I mean, I'm still pretty hyper.*

TEACHER: *And you'd get in trouble for that stuff?*

STUDENT: *Yup. No point in coming to school just to get in trouble.*

TEACHER: *And the work you couldn't do . . . was that just work that involved reading, or other things too?*

STUDENT: *Well, there's reading in almost everything at school. Except for, like, PE and lunch.*

TEACHER: *I suppose that's true.*

STUDENT: *Well, math doesn't always have so much reading. I was pretty good at math.*

TEACHER: *That's good to know. So school wasn't a total wash.*

STUDENT: *What's that mean?*

TEACHER: *I mean, there were some things you were good at.*

STUDENT: *I guess . . . mostly I was good at getting into trouble.*

TEACHER: *So what would happen back then when you needed to read something?*

STUDENT: *I'd ask one of my friends what it said. Then I'd get in trouble for talking. Or I'd just walk out of the class.*

TEACHER: *And they tried to help you with the reading?*

STUDENT: *Yeah, but . . . I don't know, I think I was kinda too hyper to, like, know what they were trying to help me with.*

TEACHER: *And, I guess I could look this up, but when did you stop showing up at school?*

STUDENT: *I started skipping in, like, the fourth grade.*

TEACHER: *Did your mom know?*

STUDENT: *No. I mean, she knows I don't go to school now. She gave up trying to get me to go. Now she's just worried that she's going to get into trouble if I don't go.*

TEACHER: *I suppose she could get in trouble if you don't go. Do you worry about that?*

STUDENT: *Not really. I mean, I do show up sometimes. Plus, we move a lot, so I change schools a lot, and sometimes it takes a while for them to figure out that I'm not showing up.*

TEACHER: *And what do you do when you don't show up?*

STUDENT: *Hang out. Sleep. Watch TV.*

TEACHER: *So, this is all very good for me to know. I appreciate you telling me. Let me see if I can summarize what you've told me. It sounds like you've had trouble reading and sitting still for a very long time . . . and have received some help with the reading before, but it wasn't very helpful . . . and now you don't really see the point in showing up at school. Do I have it right?*

STUDENT: *Yep.*

TEACHER: *Is there anything else getting in the way of you showing up at school besides those things?*

STUDENT: *Well, now I stay up pretty late . . . playing video games . . . and so I don't really wake up to come to school anymore.*

TEACHER: *That's good to know too. Anything else?*

STUDENT: *Not that I can think of.*

TEACHER: *Do you think it's still hard for you to sit in class?*

STUDENT: *Not like it used to be. Plus, a lot of times when I show up, I'm just sleeping here anyway.*

TEACHER: *Yes, I've heard that from some of your other teachers. OK. Well, I have some concerns about what you've told me. Can I tell you what my concerns are?*

STUDENT: *I guess.*

TEACHER: *Well, I have a few. First, I'm really sorry reading is still so hard for you. And I'm really sorry that you didn't get the help you needed with that a long time ago.*

STUDENT: *Oh, I got help. It just didn't help.*

TEACHER: *Yes. So, that's one of my concerns. The help you got didn't help and it's still hard for you to read, and now it sounds like you've given up on reading . . . and on school in general. And my concern is that I think there might still be some ways we could help you learn things even if you're having difficulty with reading. But if you're not here, we can't help you. And if you're sleeping when you're here, we can't help you anyway. I guess my concern is that you're not going to get a high school diploma if you don't show up, and that's going to make it harder for you to get a job.*

STUDENT: *Oh, there's jobs for people like me.*

TEACHER: *Well, perhaps so. But do you understand my concerns?*

STUDENT: *Uh-huh.*

TEACHER: *So, here's the thing. I don't think we can address all of your concerns with the same solution. If it's OK with you, how about we focus on your concerns about the reading. We'll talk about the other concerns another time. That OK?*

STUDENT: *Uh-huh. But I don't think you can help me with the reading. No one ever has.*

TEACHER: *Well, maybe you're right. Maybe, in the beginning, we need a solution that doesn't focus so much on the reading. I mean, reading is what's been keeping you from learning and showing up at school. I'm wondering if we can do something about the reading so it's not getting in the way for you so much.*

STUDENT: *How would we do that?*

TEACHER: *I don't know. That's what we'd need to figure out. I wonder if there's something we can do so you can learn things at school—and maybe someday get a diploma—without the reading causing you to become so discouraged that you don't even see the point in showing up. Do you have any ideas?*

STUDENT: *Well, I don't want to be in a special reading class. That's embarrassing. And it doesn't work anyway. And I don't want the whole world knowing I can't read. I wish I could learn stuff without doing the reading.*

TEACHER: *Hmmm. Interesting thought.*

STUDENT: *Really?*

TEACHER: *Yeah, really. Believe it or not, that might be possible. But if we're going to help you learn things without having to read, we'd need to do it in a way that doesn't embarrass you and doesn't let the whole world know you have trouble with reading. Yes?*

STUDENT: *Yes.*

TEACHER: *And no special reading class.*

STUDENT: *Right.*

TEACHER: *Any thoughts on how we could do that?*

STUDENT: *No.*

TEACHER: *Well, let's think about it.*

STUDENT: *Antonio gets help from that guy who comes in and tutors kids. What's his name?*

TEACHER: *I think you mean Mr. Hartt.*

STUDENT: *Yeah, old guy?*

TEACHER: *Well, I guess he's kind of old. You'd be open to having Mr. Hartt help you?*

STUDENT: *Yeah, but, like you said, not with reading. With learning.*

TEACHER: *You'd be OK with him teaching you stuff and reading some things to you?*

STUDENT: *But not in front of everybody.*

TEACHER: *He meets with kids in the conference room in the office. It's very private.*

STUDENT: *I guess we could try that.*

TEACHER: *I'll have to look into what his schedule is . . . and see if Mrs. Conant will approve it.*

STUDENT: *How come we have to talk to Mrs. Conant about it?*

TEACHER: *Because she has to approve anything we do that's not in the classroom.*

STUDENT: *She's who suspends me.*

TEACHER: *Yes, I suppose she is. Well, I guess she's just been following the rules. But I know she very badly wants to see if there's a way for us to have you showing up and learning . . . so I'm betting she'll try hard to make this work. And we have a few other things to figure out . . . like how much time you'll be spending with Mr. Hartt—if he can do it—and how much time you'll still be in class. So I think we also have to get Mr. Perkins involved, because he would have to approve the plan too. And he might have some other ideas for help we could give you.*

STUDENT: *I don't know him.*

TEACHER: *Well, he's not a teacher . . . he supervises all the programs of kids who need different kinds of help. But I know he'll want to make sure we have a plan that works for you.*

STUDENT: *So we have to meet again.*

TEACHER: *Yes, at least one more time. Plus, there are other parts of this problem we still need to solve. So I don't think we can come up with a complete plan today. But here's my other concern: I don't know when I can get Mr. Perkins to meet with us because I don't know his schedule. And if you're not showing up, you won't be here to meet with him.*

STUDENT: *Can't I just meet with you?*

TEACHER: *Um . . . I suppose I could talk to Mr. Perkins myself and then let you know what he says. Today is Wednesday . . . and I'm betting I won't be able to get ahold of him until tomorrow. Can you be sure to be here on Friday?*

STUDENT: *I'll try.*

TEACHER: *That would be great.*

So that problem isn't quite solved, not yet anyway. Students who aren't showing up at school often have large piles of accumulated unsolved problems, and they aren't all going to get solved in the first Plan B. On the bright side, the student did participate in the discussion; the teacher obtained a lot of information; and the student stayed engaged as they discussed potential solutions. Will she show up on Friday for the next discussion? Maybe, maybe not. Will the discussion continue the next time she does show up? Yes. All problem solving is incremental. Plan B is a process.

Q & A

Question: It's a Plan A world. How does Plan B help a kid live in The Real World?

Answer: It's not a Plan A world. Although The Real World most definitely has expectations, it doesn't impose solutions anywhere nearly as often as people think it does. More often, The Real World demands that a person identify and articulate her concerns, take the concerns of others into account, generate alternative solutions, and solve problems in a realistic and mutually satisfactory manner. Those are skills trained with Plan B. The reason you're using Plan B is to teach the kid the skills she lacks so that she can handle problems she'll face in The Real World, just as you would with any other developmental delay. Plan A doesn't do that.

> *The reason you're using Plan B is to teach the kid the skills she lacks so that she can handle problems she'll face in The Real World, just as you would with any other developmental delay. Plan A doesn't do that.*

Question: I guess I've been thinking—or at least acting like—the most important role I can play in the lives of my students is to push them harder if they aren't meeting my expectations. But a lot of them just push back. I'm starting to recognize that although there's been a lot of pushing, there hasn't been much problem solving going on. Safe to assume that pushing isn't my best role?

Answer: Not if you're interested in figuring out what's been making it hard for some of your students to meet your expectations and helping them overcome those hurdles. Having high expectations is a wonderful thing, especially if your students can meet those expectations. But if a student is having difficulty meeting an expectation, pushing won't help you identify why, won't help you partner with the student in solving the problem, and won't solve it. Your best role as a helper is problem solver, not pusher.

Question: For how long do we have to do Plan B with a kid?

Answer: Plan B isn't a temporary fix to help you eventually return to Plan A. It's a way to engage kids in solving the problems that affect their lives. It's a way to help them meet the expectations of The Real World. Why would you stop doing Plan B?

Question: Is it OK to have a specific behavior be the focus of Plan B? Like, for example, hitting?

Answer: It's not ideal. Remember, if you try to talk with a student about her challenging behavior, she's likely to think she's in trouble, likely to become defensive, and less likely to participate in the discussion. Also, if you talk with her about a behavior, you are, in effect, simultaneously talking with her about all the unsolved problems that cause that behavior. Better to figure out what unsolved problems are setting the stage for the student to hit and try to solve those problems. Then she won't be hitting in response to them anymore.

Question: What if the kid doesn't follow through on her part of the solution?

Answer: It probably wasn't realistic and/or mutually satisfactory in the first place. Back to Plan B to figure out why the solution didn't accomplish the mission so that it can be refined or replaced with a solution that comes closer to the mark. Remember, you don't want to sign off on a solution until you and the student have given conscious, deliberate thought to whether it's truly realistic and truly addresses the concerns of both parties. Don't get so excited that a solution has been proposed that you sign off on it instantaneously. All solutions are evaluated on the basis of whether they're realistic and mutually satisfactory. That's the litmus test.

Question: What if the solutions a kid proposes are not realistic or mutually satisfactory?

Answer: That's not an uncommon scenario for people—not just kids—who haven't had a whole lot of practice coming up with realistic and mutually satisfactory solutions and may be accustomed to power struggles. So she'll need some feedback along those lines. Such feedback might sound like this: *"Hey, there's an idea. The only problem is, I don't know if it's truly realistic for us to assume that you'll be able to make it through the entire school year without interacting with Catherine. Let's see if we can come up with a solution that you can really do."* Or *"Well, I suppose one option would be for you to just skip doing your math homework. And I guess that would address your concerns. But it wouldn't really address my concern that I really want you to get some extra practice at what we're covering in math. Let's see if we can come up with a solution that works for both of us."* In general, kids don't respond badly at all to such feedback, especially since it's being delivered in the context of a collaborative partnership.

Question: I agreed on a solution with one of my students, and it was working well for a few weeks; then it stopped working. What happened?

Answer: Although it could be that the solution you and the kid agreed on wasn't as realistic and mutually satisfactory as it originally seemed, it could also be that the original solution addressed only the concerns you heard about in the initial Plan B, but didn't (and couldn't) address concerns you *didn't* hear about. Head back to Plan B to see if you missed something. And it could also be that your initial success was due more to the quick burst of relationship enhancing that often occurs with Plan B. So it wasn't the solution working for you, it was the improved relationship. Although improved relationships are certainly a wonderful thing, realistic and mutually satisfactory solutions are even more wonderful.

Question: Should a student be punished if the solution doesn't work?

Answer: Why would you punish the student? Didn't you both agree on the solution?

Question: What if the kid says she doesn't care about my concern?

Answer: You need to find out what she means. Maybe she's had a lot of her concerns blown off the table and is now responding in kind. Maybe "I don't care" is something the kid says almost automatically in response to perceived criticism or when she feels like she's in trouble or on the spot. The long-term answer to a kid not caring about your concerns is to find out and care more about hers.

> *The long-term answer to a kid not caring about your concerns is to find out and care more about hers.*

Question: I have a classroom full of kids whose unsolved problems have been stacked up for a long time. I get that now. And I get that I need to do an ALSUP and that I need to get my priorities straight for each of them. And I get that solving those problems is going to take time. But what do I do about all the other problems while I'm working on my priorities?

Answer: Great question. Don't forget about Plan C. Early on, you may need to structure your classroom so that a meaningful number of expectations are set aside, at least for now. Doing that may not sound feasible, but your other option is even less appealing: continuing to have lots of expectations that a meaningful number of your students can't meet. Remember, you inherited many of those unsolved problems. The reason the unsolved problems are stacked so high is that they haven't been solved—or even identified—previously. It's going to take a while to shake things out, and that's not going happen in one fell swoop. You're doing your students an enormous favor by structuring your classroom in a way that permits lots of problem solving and doesn't impose expectations that your students can't meet. And, eventually, a lot of those unmet expectations will start getting met.

Question: I'm having trouble imagining doing Plan B with kids younger than seven or eight years old.

Answer: Don't sell those preschoolers short! They have unsolved problems, they have concerns about those unsolved problems, and they are frequently able to participate in the process of solving the problems that affect their lives. The key variable is language-processing skills, not chronological age. I've worked with three-year-olds who were able to participate in Plan B more easily than some of the seventeen-year-olds with whom I've worked.

Question: Does CPS help with kids on the autism spectrum? The ones who almost always get applied behavior analysis (ABA)?

Answer: The autism spectrum represents an extraordinarily wide range of functioning. The term "autism spectrum" tells us nothing about a student's capacity to participate in the process of solving the problems that affect her life. Again the most common obstacle is communication skills, and there are kids with communication skill delays who aren't on the autism spectrum. There are many ways (besides verbal give-and-take) to help a kid communicate about her concerns and participate in the process of contemplating and selecting solutions: pictures, sign language, hand signals, and so forth. If we're only relying on adult observations and solutions, we're depriving kids of the opportunity to practice solving problems, which makes them completely dependent on adults for solutions to those problems, and deprives adults of information about the kids' concerns. No matter how "low functioning" a child may be, we should always be cognizant of opportunities to engage her in solving problems. Dependence on adults is not a characteristic we want to promote. By the way, there's a lot more similarity between CPS and some forms of ABA than you might think. The key is whether adults are seeking information from the child (rather than relying solely on observations of behavior to draw conclusions) and involving the child in the process of arriving at solutions (rather than having adults assuming total responsibility for deciding on solutions and incentivizing compliance).

Question: Are there kids Plan B won't help, who really need to be placed in programs outside of public schools?

Answer: There will always be kids who, despite our best efforts, will need to be placed in such programs. But the reason so many kids are being placed in such programs these days—at great cost—is the large piles of unsolved problems and the extreme behaviors that are being caused by those unsolved problems. Plan B is free and, in combination with Plan C, has kept a lot of kids in their home schools.

Question: Aren't there some behaviorally challenging kids who need meds?

Answer: Yes, though nowhere near as many as are actually on meds. There are some things medication can be expected to address and things medication should not be expected to address. If we aren't aware of that differentiation, we'll see a lot of kids end up on medication for things that medication doesn't address, often because caregivers aren't sure what else to do. Now you know what else to do. Medicine is effective at reducing hyperactivity and poor impulse control, improving attention span, enhancing mood, reducing obsessive-compulsive behaviors and anxiety, reducing tics, inducing sleep, and helping volatile, aggressive kids be less reactive. There are some kids for whom medication is an indispensable aspect of treatment and who are unable to benefit from Plan B without pharmacological help. But medicine does not teach skills, and medication does not solve problems.

> *There are some kids for whom medication is an indispensable aspect of treatment. . . . but medicine does not teach skills, and medication does not solve problems.*

EXPERIENCE IS THE BEST TEACHER

"So much of what we do as educators is assess the situation and decide on a solution . . . that's what teachers are accustomed to doing. And what we've learned is that we're not always accurate in what we assume to be the reasons behind why kids do things. Having those conversations with the kids has been a huge eye-opener. The essence of solving problems collaboratively is that the student has voice and choice in the situation. Look at the process. First we listen to them. We gather information. It's about listening, but it's also about asking the right questions. And then the adult shares his or her concerns, and then the two work together to solve problems. That parallels a lot of the cutting-edge work on academic instruction these days. So I've been lucky to see this kind of unique connection between CPS and very progressive, research-based, modern instruction."

—TOM, ASSISTANT SUPERINTENDENT

"Once you really start using CPS, you realize how much it's connected to the curriculum and to classroom management techniques. You can read anything on curriculum and instruction, and the research is talking about things that are connected to CPS. It's been wonderful to see—that all parts of the school are connected with CPS's philosophy that *kids do well if they can.* Getting kids' perspective is the overarching goal for all of us."

—NINA, PRINCIPAL

"When we actually began doing Plan B with kids, really putting it into action, some found it a bit intimidating because people aren't used to having those real, deep conversations with kids about what the child is experiencing."

—RYAN, ASSISTANT PRINCIPAL

"One of my kids last year was having difficulty moving on to a different math station. She kept going back to working again on whatever the activity was in the last station. So I just said, 'Well, you know, I noticed that you had some difficulty during math yesterday. What's up?' She said, 'I wasn't good at it. I got it wrong. I'm not the best at math anymore.' And I said, 'Oh. So missing the problem made you think that you weren't good at math?' And she said, 'Yeah.' I asked her for more, and she said, 'Well, I don't like that people think I can't do it.' I said, 'So what I'm hearing is that when you miss something, you think people will think that you can't do it?' She said, 'Yeah, they won't think I'm smart.' So eventually we got to talking about solutions. She likes challenging problems. So we talked about the fact that she could do math work that's easy for her or math work that's challenging, but that if she does the challenging work, it's probably going to be harder, and she's probably going to make some mistakes. And she agreed that she still wanted to do the challenging work, but that she'd let me know if she needed help instead of putting her head on the desk because she's worried that people won't think she's smart. I was surprised, because I thought she was going to just say she was frustrated when she couldn't get it. I was really surprised to learn she was worried people weren't going to think she was smart."

—Kathy, teacher

"We're usually wrong about kids' concerns."

—Katie, learning center teacher

"I did Plan B with a student on his difficulties coming into school in the morning. He was having trouble separating from his mom. I remember thinking that he needed a checklist in the morning; you know, like, 'Put my backpack up. Check. Take my boots off. Check.' But that solution made no sense once we heard what his concerns were. I think he said something like, 'There's just too many people in the classroom in the morning.' I had never even thought of that! I learned that when you do Plan B, you hear things you didn't expect. And the solution was as simple as him just saying that it would work better for him if he could just wait for a little bit for everyone else to come into the classroom. And then as soon as the other kids went in, he would go in and do everything. He didn't need that checklist."

—Katie, learning center teacher

"And sometimes the kids' solutions don't make sense to adults either. I was doing Plan B with two kids who were fighting over the same doll. The solution they came up with was that one of them would play with it for ten minutes and the other would play with it for fifteen. It wasn't equal. But they were good with the solution, even though it made no sense to me."

—Vicki, director of communications

❝There was another student who had difficulty coming to school, and he was basically pretty oppositional about doing anything all day. And so I started off Plan B with, 'I've noticed that it's been difficult for you to come to school. What's up?' What I learned is that he didn't want to leave his Legos. Did I expect to hear that? No. Turns out he'd been working on the Legos all summer, and he was in the middle of a project and didn't want to leave the Legos. So we agreed that when he was finished with the project, he'd either bring it in or bring in some pictures to share with the class. He brought in some pictures, and that was the start of hooking him in. We did a lot of Plan B that year. His dad came in at the end of the school year and said to me, 'We can't believe how he's getting up in the morning and he wants to go to school. He's talking at the dinner table about his school day. It's such a change!' I said, 'He's worked really, really hard, and I'm so glad to hear this.' And then his dad got teary-eyed and said, 'I wish that I'd had this when I was in school, because I think it would have made all the difference for me.' Then he gave me a big hug, and I realized this is really about changing people's lives.

The student doesn't need much Plan B anymore. It sounds awful to be excited about that, but there haven't been very many problems to solve anymore. The reason that's exciting is that everybody was worried that kids would become dependent on the help. You know, how's he going to make it in the real world? But once the skills are taught, the kids have a better shot at making it in the real world.

His parents were so frustrated about what was going on at school in the beginning. I can remember the earlier meetings, and they were at a total loss for what to do. They were trying everything. They were being really strict. They were taking things away. And we said, 'Oh, please don't do that.' They came to trust us.❞

—KATHY, SECOND – GRADE TEACHER

❝We had a kid who was like a caveman in the beginning. He barely spoke. His hair was always over his face. Didn't have much language. Just grunting. He was just like the Tasmanian Devil. Just running around, bumping into things, ripping things apart—completely out of control. His mom had drug abuse issues. She told us at an IEP meeting that she didn't do discipline, or structure, or whatever. He told me that his dad was in jail for murdering someone, which wasn't correct. It was for domestic abuse. But this kid was completely out of control. The student just hadn't been socialized at all.

People told me, 'You need to get shin guards or something because you're getting kicked,' and everything like that. But we nurtured him, and we accepted him, and slowly but surely we started to have some expectations for him. And gradually he started meeting them. He began to trust us.**"**

—ANONYMOUS, EDUCATIONAL TECHNICIAN

"This is a kid that everyone said needed to be placed out of district. Everyone said that this kid should not be in public school. He should be in residential care or day treatment. Now that we know him, we know how smart he is. Now, 99 percent of his time is in class. He's able to verbalize when he needs help. And it was a transformation for the mother. She's working with us. She trusts us completely.**"**

—NINA, PRINCIPAL

"What's been fantastic about CPS is it's been helping us with those kids that we couldn't figure out. You don't understand why they continue to make the same mistakes again and again—you're not sure what the concerns are. This process has been unbelievably helpful with those kids.**"**

—RYAN, ASSISTANT PRINCIPAL

"Something that struck me the most about CPS is how, over time, it took the tension and anger away from kids that I worked with when teachers referred them to the office for help. Students knew that I cared for them, that I would listen to them, and that they had a voice in the process. At the same time, they also knew that the school has expectations and concerns for them and all students. They still had lagging skills, which could still make life challenging, but their 'calmness' allowed for more productive and solution-based interactions between everyone to address those problems.**"**

—RYAN, ASSISTANT PRINCIPAL

CHAPTER 7

THE PITFALLS

First attempts at Plan B often don't go very well. You're new at it; the kid's new at it, too. Creating a helping relationship and using Plan B effectively take time, practice, and perseverance. So hang in there. Feeling like you have your Plan B sea legs under you can take a while. Here are some of the common problems that people run into early (and sometimes later) on.

YOU'RE NOT ACTUALLY USING PLAN B

Plan B is definitely harder if you're really doing Plan A. Sometimes people use Plan A instead of Plan B because they found themselves stuck in the middle of an incompatibility episode and felt they had to take decisive, unilateral action. The ALSUP and Problem Solving Plan should help you keep those scenarios to a minimum. Remember, *once an unsolved problem has set in motion an incompatibility episode for the first time, it's no longer unpredictable.*

As such, it can be handled proactively (and preferably collabora-tively). That's why those two instruments are so important.

Another reason adults use Plan A instead of Plan B is that they still think Plan A is going to accomplish something positive. Of course, if Plan A were working, you wouldn't still be using it so often.

> *Early Plan B discussions can be uncomfortable; it's new for you and for the student. But every Plan B yields important information, even if it doesn't flow seamlessly.*

Sometimes adults default to Plan A when, in the midst of doing Plan B, they feel uncertain or stuck and revert to something more familiar. Early Plan B discussions can be uncomfortable; it's new for you and for the student. But every Plan B yields important informa-tion, even if it doesn't flow seamlessly.

Adults may also revert to Plan A in the midst of Plan B because they're a lot more focused on *their* concerns (and perhaps their solutions) than they are on the kid's concerns. Maybe it's just hu-man nature to be more focused on your own concern than that of another person. And maybe many adults had a lot of practice having their concerns ignored or dismissed in childhood and ad-olescence and are simply perpetuating the cycle. But when you're using Plan B, you're as focused on clarifying and addressing the kid's concerns as you are on clarifying and addressing your own concerns.

And sometimes adults are still using Plan A because they still think the overriding agenda is to teach the kid who's the boss. But he already knows you're the boss. What he's looking for is some-one to help him solve the problems that are contributing to the challenging behaviors that are causing (some) adults to believe that he needs additional lessons on who's the boss, and that the hundreds of lessons he's already received on that theme haven't yet sunk in.

Watch a school administrator make a few common Plan B errors. Go to http://livesinthebalance.org/step-three-fifth-video.

BAD TIMING

Plan B is, without question, a lot harder if you're trying to use it emergently. Proactive Plan B takes place under planned conditions, so you have time to prepare. Proactive Plan B takes place under calmer, less heated circumstances, so the participants are more capable of information sharing and reasoned discussion. And Proactive Plan B doesn't take place in front of the entire class, so the participants don't have the added pressure of being the center of attention, and the work of the other kids isn't being disrupted.

It's not that the use of Emergency Plan B is a catastrophe; it's just that you don't want to make a habit of it. If you're trying to solve the same problem every day using Emergency Plan B, you're actually doing more Plan B than is necessary. Remember, the goal is to work toward durable solutions—getting the problem solved once and for all—a task much better suited to Proactive Plan B.

But here's an example of an Emergency Plan B that went pretty well. It took place as a teacher was walking with students down the hallway to reading class, and noticing that one student—it happened to be one of her behaviorally challenging kids—looked quite unhappy:

TEACHER: *What's the matter, Matt?*

MATT: *I don't like my new reading partner.*

TEACHER: *You don't like your new reading partner.*

MATT: *No. Mrs. Dunleavy changed our reading partners yesterday, and I got stuck with Melanie.*

TEACHER: *Ah, I didn't know that. So you don't want Melanie as your reading partner.*

MATT: *No way! Why'd she stick me with Melanie?*

TEACHER: *I don't know . . . though I did know that you and Melanie don't get along very well.*

MATT: *Well, it's going to ruin reading.*

TEACHER: *I'm glad you told me about this, Matt. And I want to make sure we get this solved so that you don't feel that reading is going to be ruined. What do you think we can do—just for today—and then later, me and you and Mrs. Dunleavy can sit down and figure something out?*

MATT: *I don't know.*

TEACHER: *Well, think for a second. Sometimes you don't think of a solution right away, but then you come up with one.*

MATT: *How 'bout I read myself today and then we talk to Mrs. Dunleavy.*

TEACHER: *So you'd read by yourself today . . . who would be Melanie's partner?*

MATT: *I don't know. She could read by herself too. Or she could join someone else's group.*

TEACHER: *Well, let's see if either of those solutions work for Mrs. Dunleavy—just for today—and I'll see if there's a time for us to meet to talk about it before tomorrow.*

MATT: *We don't have reading group again until Friday.*

TEACHER: *Oh, right, so we have more time than I thought. You good with this plan, just for today?*

MATT: *Uh-huh.*

By the way, Plan A could make sense in some emergent circumstances, especially those involving safety, when there's no viable option except to impose adult will (for example, if two kids are in the midst of a fistfight). But on many emergent safety issues, you do still have the options of Plans B and C. Plan C would make sense when you think defusing a student (by dropping the expectation that heated him up in the first place) is feasible, such as when a student suddenly balks at getting to work on a particular assignment. But, again, if we're doing a good job of identifying the lagging skills and unsolved problems of kids at risk for unsafe behavior, if we're working together to communicate and prioritize, if we're systematically solving those problems and keeping track of how things are going, if we're developing the types of helping relationships with at-risk kids that they so desperately need, then the likelihood of unsafe behavior will already have been dramatically reduced.

When I'm told that Plan B didn't work—that the kid didn't talk—I often ask the adults involved in the Plan B to tell me the story. Often the story begins with the words, *"Well, when he . . ."* This is usually a clear sign that *Emergency* Plan B was at work. I'm always encouraging the adults to go back and do Plan B on the unsolved problem, but proactively instead of emergently. In the vast majority of circumstances, that usually does the trick.

PERFUNCTORY INFORMATION GATHERING

This refers to the tendency to rush through the Empathy step as quickly as possible, which causes adults to have only a partial understanding of the kid's concern or perspective. Thus, instead of fully clarifying the kid's concern, a "low-quality concern" is settled for in the interest of expedience. The problem, of course, is that *mushy concerns lead to mushy solutions. If the kid's concerns are not well specified, it's unlikely that the eventual solution will address his actual concerns.*

> *Mushy concerns lead to mushy solutions. If the kid's concerns are not well specified, it's unlikely that the eventual solution will address his actual concerns.*

Many adults find it hard to stay patient in the Empathy step. But the goal is not to get the conversation done in a nanosecond (another good reason to be using Proactive B rather than Emergency B). Problems that get solved in a nanosecond usually aren't durably solved. Again, you're not done with the Empathy step until you have the clearest possible understanding of the kid's concern or perspective.

In one of the videos I show at my trainings, a wonderful elementary school teacher named Dorothy Plumpton is doing Proactive Plan B with one of her students, Bobby. The unsolved problem is that Bobby was having difficulty sitting on the floor during group lessons. The first concern Bobby articulated was that the buttons on the back of his pants might bother him. The second concern was that the floor was dirty. Fortunately, Mrs. Plumpton didn't stop there. She learned about a variety of additional concerns: that there was too much noise in the classroom, that one of Bobby's classmates was whispering in his ear, that he was frequently blamed for things he didn't do. She also learned that he was fine sitting on the floor in writing group, that he was fine reading to himself in reading group, but that he didn't like reading out loud in reading group because other kids teased classmates who made mistakes in reading out loud during reading group. If Mrs. Plumpton had stopped drilling after the first two concerns, she would have tried addressing the buttons on Bobby's pants and the dirt on the floor, but would never have known about Bobby's other concerns, in which case the problem would have remained unsolved.

See educators Aliscia Krecisz, Dorothy Plumpton, Dave DiGiacomo, and Kate Thurman discuss their experiences with the CPS model. Go to http://livesinthebalance.org/voices-solving-problems-collaboratively.

TOO MUCH INFORMATION

That last example brings to the fore another problem that can arise in the Empathy step: the kid talked *a lot*, and you obtained what felt like an overwhelming amount of information. Believe it or not, this is a good problem to have, kind of like having too many good players on your basketball team and wondering which ones to put in the game. But it does raise an important logistical issue: deciding which concerns to address in the current Plan B discussion. If we use Bobby and Mrs. Plumpton as our example, it's quite clear that one solution couldn't possibly address all of Bobby's concerns (that is, whatever solution might address the dirt on the floor wouldn't address kids giving each other a hard time if they made a mistake when they're reading out loud). So, before moving on to the next two steps, Bobby and Mrs. Plumpton would have to decide which concerns to address in the current Plan B and which to save for subsequent Plan B discussions.

How do you know when you're done gathering information in the Empathy step? Again, keep using drilling strategy number 8—summarizing—until the kid can't think of any other concerns. By the way, you'll know whether you've done a good job of identifying and clarifying concerns when you try to restate the concerns of both parties in the Invitation. If you have trouble restating those concerns, there's a decent chance you're still lacking important information. What should you do then? Go back to the first two steps and see if there's more information to be had. Your other option is to plunge forward with mushy concerns, and you know what kind of solutions you're going to end up with if you do that.

> *You'll know whether you've done a good job of identifying and clarifying concerns when you try to restate the concerns of both parties in the Invitation. If you have trouble restating those concerns, there's a decent chance you're still lacking important information.*

THE KID WOULDN'T TALK

You've already read about many of the reasons kids don't talk in the Empathy step, so this is a recap. First, your unsolved problem may have been poorly worded. Second, your timing may have been off. Another possibility is that many kids aren't clear about what their concerns are. Because kids are accustomed to having their concerns dismissed, it's possible they haven't given the matter much thought. They may need some help getting a bead on their concerns. Good drilling should help here; but if the kid truly has no clue about his concerns, your best strategy would be *educated guessing* or *hypothesis testing.* Your powers of observation and recollection of past instances in which the child (or others) had a similar problem should serve you well here. Plus, there are only a finite number of concerns or problems that might be associated with a given unmet expectation.

Bear in mind that your educated guesses are *tentative hypotheses.* You want to make sure it's the *kid's* actual concerns, and not your presuppositions, that are entered into consideration. If your educated guess is on the money or even close, kids will usually find a way to let you know. And they'll let you know if your guess is off base, too. Here's another example of what educated guessing might sound like:

ADULT, INITIATING PROACTIVE PLAN B: *I've noticed that sometimes you have difficulty standing in line during lunch. What's up?*

STUDENT: *I don't know.*

ADULT: *Take your time. There's no rush. Think about it a little. What's hard for you about standing in line for lunch?*

STUDENT: *(shrugs)*

ADULT: *Picture yourself in the lunch line and think about what might be hard for you about that.*

STUDENT: *I'm not sure.*

ADULT, EDUCATED GUESSING: *Well, I was wondering if it has anything to do with who's standing in front of you or behind you. Could that be it?*

STUDENT: *I don't think so.*

ADULT: *OK. I think one time you were upset because they didn't have what you wanted when you got to the servers. Is that something you're concerned about when you're standing in line?*

STUDENT: *Yes.*

ADULT: *So you're worried that they might not have what you want?*

STUDENT: *Sometimes they run out. And then I have to eat something I don't like.*

ADULT: *I see. That's good for me to know. So what do you do when you're worried that they might run out of what you want?*

STUDENT: *I try to go ahead in the line to see if they're running out. And then everyone gets mad at me because they think I'm trying to cut the line. But I'm not trying to cut the line; I'm just trying to see if they're running out. But then the lunch lady gets mad because the other kids are hollering about me cutting the line.*

ADULT: *Goodness, I didn't know anything about this. Although I have heard about a few incidents from Mrs. Gorman. But now I have a much better understanding of what's going on. Tell me, is there anything else making it hard to stand in line at lunch?*

STUDENT: *Sometimes Danny flicks my ear, so I don't want to stand in front of him.*

ADULT: *Ah, so maybe my first idea is sometimes true. The part about who's standing in front or behind you.*

STUDENT: *Only in back of me. And only Danny.*

ADULT: *Got it. Anything else I should know about what's hard about standing in line for lunch?*

STUDENT: *I can't think of anything else.*

ADULT: *I can't either. But at least now we have an idea of what's making that hard for you.*

FEAR OF FABRICATION

It's not uncommon for adults to conclude that a kid's concerns aren't "accurate" or that he's lying. We're usually wrong about that. Lying is what a kid does when you're asking about his *behavior* and he thinks he's in trouble. But you're not asking about his behavior and he's not in trouble. Although some students fabricate because of embarrassment over their true concerns—a fairly rare occurrence, in my experience—there's really very little for a student to lie about in the Empathy step, since all you're looking for is information about his concern, perspective, or point of view.

It's also important to be open to the possibility that your own assumptions about the kid's concerns are inaccurate. Just because the kid's concerns didn't coincide with what *you* thought his concerns would be doesn't mean he's lying. Along these lines, there are basically two mistakes you can make:

1. Assuming the kid's concerns are accurate when there's a chance they're not
2. Assuming the kid's concerns are not accurate when there's a chance the kid has hit the nail on the head

> *Accusing a kid of fabricating—or expressing skepticism about the accuracy or authenticity of his concerns— can be fatal to the information-gathering process of the Empathy step.*

The first mistake is far preferable. The price of the second mistake is much higher. Accusing a kid of fabricating—or expressing skepticism about the accuracy or authenticity of his concerns— can be fatal to the information-gathering process of the Empathy step. In other words, it causes kids—like the rest of us—to clam up or become defensive. Good drilling should eventually help you get past any potential inaccuracies and clarify the kid's concerns anyway.

The worst-case scenario, and this is no tragedy, is that you and the kid agree to a solution that addresses the kid's stated concern (but not what turns out to be the primary or central concern), and the original solution doesn't resolve the problem. When you return to Plan B, you want to suggest that there might be more to the problem than was captured by your original discussion. Here's an example of how Mrs. Plumpton might return to Plan B if the first type of mistake I described were to play out:

TEACHER: *Bobby, remember when we talked about how it was hard for you to sit in reading group because there's dirt on the floor?*
BOBBY: *Uh-huh.*
TEACHER: *And remember that we decided that you'd sit in a chair instead?*
BOBBY: *Uh-huh.*
TEACHER: *Well, I've noticed that it's still been hard for you to be in reading group. So I'm beginning to wonder if there are other reasons you're having difficulty sitting in reading group. Can we think about that a little?*

SOMETHING'S MISSING

You definitely don't want to skip any of the steps. Each of the three steps is absolutely indispensable for solving problems collaboratively. If you skip the Empathy step, you won't know what the student's concerns are, and those concerns won't get addressed. If you skip the Define Adult Concerns step, the student won't know what your concerns are, and they won't get addressed. And if you skip the Invitation, you won't work together in coming up with a realistic and mutually satisfactory solution.

PLAYING ROULETTE WITH THE STEPS

Plan B doesn't go very well if you apply the steps out of order. If you start with the Define Adult Concerns step, the kid's going to think you're doing Plan A (because Plan A starts with your concerns, followed rapidly by your imposed solutions). If you start with the Invitation, you have no idea what problem you're trying to solve because you haven't yet identified anyone's concerns. Plan

B always starts with the Empathy step, continues with the Define Adult Concerns step, and is capped off with the Invitation.

THE STUDENT COULDN'T THINK OF ANY SOLUTIONS

It's not uncommon for kids to have difficulty thinking of realistic and mutually satisfactory solutions in the Invitation. Of course, many adults have difficulty coming up with realistic and mutually satisfactory solutions too. Fortunately, even though you're giving the kid the first crack at the solution, coming up with a solution is a team effort. If he doesn't have any ideas, maybe you do. Remember, any proposals you make in the solution department are just that: *proposals*. If you're *imposing* solutions, you're using Plan A.

THE FIRST SOLUTION DIDN'T GET THE JOB DONE

First solutions frequently don't get the job done, so you're likely to run into this. Why wouldn't the first solution get the job done? As you've read, one possibility is that the solution wasn't as realistic as you and the kid thought it was. That's not a Plan B failure, just a solution that wasn't as realistic as it seemed. Go back to Plan B to come up with a more realistic solution. Another possibility is that the solution wasn't as mutually satisfactory as it seemed. That's not a Plan B failure either, just a solution that wasn't as mutually satisfactory as it seemed. Go back to Plan B to figure out why and refine the original solution or come up with one that better addresses the concerns of both parties. It's also possible that you identified as many concerns as possible in the first attempt at Plan B on a given unsolved problem and came up with a solution that addressed those concerns. But there are concerns the solution didn't address: the ones you didn't identify. That's not a Plan B failure, just a scenario in which there were more concerns to be addressed than was initially thought. Go back to Plan B to see if there are other concerns that the original solution didn't address.

> *At the end of Plan B—after you and the kid have signed off on a solution and given conscious, deliberate thought to whether the solution is realistic and mutually satisfactory—it's good to acknowledge that the problem may require additional discussion.*

At the end of Plan B—after you and the kid have signed off on a solution and given conscious, deliberate thought to whether the solution is realistic and mutually satisfactory—it's good to acknowledge that the problem may require additional discussion. Good solutions—durable ones—are often refined versions of the solutions that came before them.

DO-OVERS

You've now learned quite a bit about the three steps of Plan B, read a few sample Plan B dialogues, and begun digesting the different ways in which things can go awry. Let's take what we've covered so far and incorporate it all into another dialogue. In this example, you'll be seeing some of the common missteps (many of which you've already read about) that can cause things to go off the rails, but you'll also be seeing how to get things back on track. In this scenario, an assistant principal is facilitating a Plan B discussion with a middle school student (Jason) and his science teacher (Ms. Bradbury).

ASSISTANT PRINCIPAL: *So, Jason, the reason I asked you and Ms. Bradbury to meet with me is because I've been seeing a lot of you in the office lately and—don't take this personally—I wouldn't mind seeing less of you. And Ms. Bradbury would really appreciate it if you weren't disrupting her science lab anymore.*

Looks like we need to take a do-over right from the start here. The assistant principal started Plan B with challenging behavior, and that's going to reduce the likelihood that Jason will participate in the conversation. Let's try again.

Do-Over:

ASSISTANT PRINCIPAL: *So, thanks for meeting with me. I thought it would be good for us to try solving a problem together. Jason, you're not in trouble . . . I just want to get your perspective on the problem we're going to be discussing, because we're not going to be able to solve it without you. We good?*

JASON: *Uh-huh.*

ASSISTANT PRINCIPAL: *But we also need Ms. Bradbury, because we need her perspective on things as well. So here's the problem I thought we could work on together, at least as I understand it: difficulty completing the lab reports in science. Ms. Bradbury, can you expand on that a little?*

MS. BRADBURY: *Well, it's all the clowning around that we just can't have happening. That's why I have to separate him from his lab partner, Chris, or send him to the office.*

That was going rather well, until the "clowning around" part. It sure is hard to keep the challenging behavior out of the discussion! Let's take another do-over:

Do-Over:

MS. BRADBURY: *Well, the expectation that Jason is having difficulty meeting is completing the science lab reports while he's seated next to his lab partner, Chris.*

ASSISTANT PRINCIPAL: *OK, so, Jason, what can you tell us about that?*

JASON: *I don't know. I mean, I don't know if I'm allowed to say this, but it's kind of boring.*

ASSISTANT PRINCIPAL: *I think we're just looking for you to be honest. So you don't want to do the science lab reports because it's boring. That's good for us to know.*

That was a nice stab at reflective listening, but Jason didn't actually say anything about not *wanting* to do the science lab reports. We want to make sure that our reflective listening comes as close as possible to what the student actually said. Let's try again.

Do-Over:

ASSISTANT PRINCIPAL: *I think we're just looking for you to be honest. So you're having difficulty completing the science lab reports because they're boring. That's good for us to know. Ms. Bradbury, why don't you tell us about your concerns about Jason having difficulty completing the science lab reports.*

Sorry to slow things down here, but we're not ready to move on to the Define Adult Concerns step just yet. We still need clarification on Jason's first concern, and we also need to find out if there are others. So there's more drilling to be done. Let's take a do-over.

Do-Over:

ASSISTANT PRINCIPAL: *I think we're just looking for you to be honest. So you're having difficulty completing the science lab reports because they're boring. That's good for us to know. But I don't think I quite understand what you mean. What's boring about them?*

JASON: *I don't know. It's just not fun. I mean, doing the experiments is pretty fun. But writing them up isn't fun. And I'm not that good at writing anyway.*

ASSISTANT PRINCIPAL: *You sure this isn't just because you'd rather socialize than do the lab reports?*

Uh-oh. An adult theory—and one related, of course, to motivation—has just been tossed into the mix. If we stick with drilling for information, we'll likely find that this theory—like most—is incorrect. Let's try again.

Do-Over:

JASON: *I don't know. It's just not fun. I mean, doing the experiments is fun. But writing them up isn't fun. And I'm not that good at writing anyway.*

ASSISTANT PRINCIPAL: *Can't Chris just do the writing for you?*

Now we're seeing that adults find it hard not only to keep behaviors and theories out of the Empathy step but also to refrain from prematurely throwing *solutions* into the mix. We really should just stick with the drilling strategies . . .

Do-Over:

JASON: *I don't know. It's just not fun. I mean, doing the experiments is pretty fun. But writing them up isn't fun. And I'm not that good at writing anyway.*

ASSISTANT PRINCIPAL: *Ah, so you're not that good at writing. Tell us more about that.*

JASON: *I'm just better at doing the experiments than I am at doing the writing. There's this whole format we're supposed to follow, and I usually get it wrong.*

ASSISTANT PRINCIPAL: *OK, so the writing part is hard because there's a format you have to follow and you usually get it wrong. Is there anything about the actual writing that's hard? Or is it mostly the format? Or both?*

JASON: *Um . . . well, I'm not very good at writing. But I think—*

MS. BRADBURY: *I think it's the format you don't like. A lot of kids don't like the format, but it's really important for you to get used to it.*

Jason was doing just fine answering for himself. We should let him continue doing that.

Do-Over:

JASON: *Um . . . well, I'm not very good at writing. But I think it's mostly the formatting part. It just makes it really confusing for me.*

ASSISTANT PRINCIPAL: *Good to know. So the formatting makes it con-fusing for you, and that makes it hard for you to complete the science lab reports. Is that separate from the boring part, or is the formatting what makes it boring?*

JASON: *Uh . . . well, writing the lab report is more boring than the experi-ment, but I think the formatting part is what makes it especially boring.*

ASSISTANT PRINCIPAL: *Got it. That's helpful. So let me summarize what we know so far . . . writing the lab report with Chris is more boring than doing the experiment, and the main thing that makes it boring is the formatting part. Yes?*

MS. BRADBURY: *And we also have the problem of you guys teasing Ilicia . . . we haven't even talked about that yet.*

Well now, moving on to a different unsolved problem really doesn't make sense here. Although it's not uncommon to stumble across new unsolved problems in the midst of the Empathy step—and although it can make sense, at times, to switch from the origi-nal unsolved problem to one of the new ones—there doesn't seem to be any reason to move off of the original unsolved problem in this instance. Let's give it another go.

Do-Over:

MS. BRADBURY: *This is good for me to know.*

ASSISTANT PRINCIPAL: *Is there anything else making it hard for you to complete the science lab reports?*

JASON: *Well, Chris is, like, making jokes the whole time. He cracks me up. So then I get in trouble for laughing.*

ASSISTANT PRINCIPAL: *OK, so Chris cracks jokes the whole time. And then you get in trouble for laughing.*

JASON: *Yeah. Well, also, sometimes I just can't stop laughing. I keep think-ing about what he said, and I just keep laughing. So that's when I get into trouble.*

MS. BRADBURY: *Yeah, I don't really mind people laughing in my class, as long as it's not disrupting the work of other students. And I don't like people fooling around when we're working with the chemicals. But that's exactly right: Jason is still laughing long after everyone else has stopped.*

JASON: *It's really hard for me to stop. I wish I could.*

ASSISTANT PRINCIPAL: *OK, so now we have two reasons that it's hard for you to complete the science lab reports with Chris. The formatting of the reports makes it hard for you to write them, and Chris says things that crack you up and it's hard for you to stop laughing. Yes?*

JASON: *Yes.*

ASSISTANT PRINCIPAL: *Anything else making it hard for you to complete the science lab reports?*

JASON: *Um . . . I can't think of anything.*

ASSISTANT PRINCIPAL: *Well, give it some more thought. No rush.*

JASON: *I don't think there's anything else.*

ASSISTANT PRINCIPAL: *Well, then, let's move on to Ms. Bradbury's concerns. Ms. Bradbury, what are your concerns about Jason having difficulty completing science lab reports?*

MS. BRADBURY: *Well, it's really important that the science lab reports get done. That's what Jason is supposed to be doing after he completes the experiment.*

That wasn't really a concern. That was simply a restatement of the expectation. Remember, adult concerns fall into one or both of two categories: (1) how the unsolved problem is affecting the student and/or (2) how the unsolved problem is affecting others. Let's try that again:

Do-Over:

MS. BRADBURY: *Well, when Jason isn't doing his lab reports, he's usually talking to other kids and getting into trouble.*

Not quite there yet. Those are the *behaviors* Jason is exhibiting when he's having difficulty completing the lab reports, but we still don't know the teacher's *concerns*. Let's try again.

Do-Over:

MS. BRADBURY: *Well, Jason, if you don't complete your lab reports, I won't know if you've grasped what you did in the experiment. And*

sometimes, when you're not doing the lab report, you're making it diffi-
cult for those around you to do theirs. Does that make sense?

JASON: *Uh-huh.*

ASSISTANT PRINCIPAL: *OK, now we have both sets of concerns identi-*
fied. So, um, Jason, I'm thinking that the best way to solve this problem
is to have you partner with someone besides Chris.

Oh, snap! Just as the threesome was about to collaborate on a solution, the assistant principal jumped back over the fence and went unilateral! Plus, that solution isn't going to address Jason's first concern, the one related to the formatting making it hard for him to do the writing. Time for a do-over.

Do-Over:

ASSISTANT PRINCIPAL: *OK, now we have both sets of concerns identi-*
fied. I don't think the same solution is going to address both sets of
concerns. So I'm thinking we may need two solutions: one for the for-
matting problem, and one for the part about Chris making you laugh.
Which one should we try solving first?

JASON: *Um . . . I don't know.*

ASSISTANT PRINCIPAL: *Ms. Bradbury, what do you think?*

MS. BRADBURY: *I don't know; they're both pretty important.*

ASSISTANT PRINCIPAL: *Well, I'm inclined to go with the formatting issue*
first. Is that OK with both of you?

JASON: *Uh-huh.*

MS. BRADBURY: *Works for me.*

ASSISTANT PRINCIPAL: *OK, so, how are you going to meet Ms. Brad-*
bury's expectations for writing the lab report? I know you can do it if
you put your mind to it!

Remember, the Invitation step should be a recap of the concerns of both parties, and that Invitation was simply a re-cap of the expectation. Recapping the concerns of both parties is really important because doing so provides a reference point for considering solutions. Plus, you want to stay away from cheerleading; enthusiasm doesn't typically solve problems. Let's try again.

Do-Over:

ASSISTANT PRINCIPAL: *How can we make writing lab reports better for you?*

Despite the good intentions, that wasn't really much closer to the mark. Remember, recapping the concerns of both parties begins with the words, "I wonder if there's a way . . ."

Do-Over:

ASSISTANT PRINCIPAL: *I wonder if there's a way for us to help you with the formatting part of the science lab reports . . . and also make sure that you can show Ms. Bradbury that you've grasped what you did in the experiment. Do you have any ideas?*

JASON: *No.*

ASSISTANT PRINCIPAL: *Take your time. There's no rush.*

JASON: *Um, could I team up with someone who's better at writing them than me? Then maybe I could learn how to do it.*

MS. BRADBURY: *Well, I do want it to be your own work. But I suppose we could do that as a starting point. Marie is very good at writing lab reports. Do you want to have her help you a little?*

JASON: *I guess.*

ASSISTANT PRINCIPAL: *OK, so let's run with that solution. Thanks guys.*

Whoa, not so fast. The litmus test for good solutions is that they be both realistic and mutually satisfactory. So we need to give conscious, deliberate thought to whether those two criteria have been satisfied. Many seemingly brilliant solutions have crashed and burned because they didn't meet the two criteria. Let's take a do-over:

Do-Over:

ASSISTANT PRINCIPAL: *Let's think about that solution. Jason, do you think that's a good way for you to learn about how to write the lab reports?*

JASON: *Yeah.*

ASSISTANT PRINCIPAL: *Ms. Bradbury, does that solution work for you?*

MS. BRADBURY: *Sure, at least in the beginning.*

ASSISTANT PRINCIPAL: *Jason, are you OK with working with Marie?*

JASON: *Not exactly. We don't really get along too well.*

ASSISTANT PRINCIPAL: *Ah, good to know. Maybe we should think of someone else?*

MS. BRADBURY: *How do you get along with Samantha?*

JASON: *Better than with Marie.*

MS. BRADBURY: *Do you want to try partnering with her instead?*

JASON: *Yeah.*

MS. BRADBURY: *But I want to make sure that Samantha isn't just doing the report for you, or that you're just replicating hers. The goal is for her to teach you how to do them, yes?*

JASON: *Yes.*

MS. BRADBURY: *And Samantha sits on the other side of the room from Chris, so maybe it'll help us with that issue as well.*

ASSISTANT PRINCIPAL: *I guess we'll find out if the laughing problem gets solved with this solution, too. In the meantime, it sounds like we have a solution to the formatting problem. You're both good with it?*

MS. BRADBURY: *Yeah. I mean, I'll need to let Samantha know that I'm switching her partner and how I hope she can help Jason with the re ports. But we switch partners every now and then anyway, so I don't think she'll mind.*

Q & A

Question: So, all of these pitfalls . . . will I ever get good at Plan B?

Answer: Well, it may seem as though there are a lot of pitfalls, but perhaps you're just reading about them for the first time. The key now is practice and reflection. After you do the Empathy step for real with a student, think about how it went. If it didn't go as well as you'd hoped, reference this chapter and figure out why. Then try again. Little by little, you'll start to feel that you have some mastery over this process. Plan B will slow down for you.

People who are new to Plan B tend to be fairly technical about it; it feels a lot more natural to people who've been doing it a while.

By the way, even if Plan B doesn't go as well as you'd hoped, something good happens in every Plan B. If you left the Empathy step prematurely, you still gathered some information, so you know more about the student's concerns than you did. Go back to the Empathy step the next day. If the solution you agreed to doesn't get the job done, at least you're partnering with a student on solutions instead of imposing your will, so the relationship- and communication-enhancing properties of Plan B are still working for you. You and the student can figure out why the original solution didn't work and come up with another one. There's really no such thing as a Plan B failure . . . just more information that still needs to be gathered and problems that haven't yet been durably solved.

Question: I'm still having difficulty getting some of my students to talk in the Empathy step. Help!

Answer: Given what you've read in this chapter, you now have a bit of a checklist for what could be getting in the way:

☐ *You're not really using Plan B; you're using Plan A.*

☐ *You're using Plan B emergently rather than proactively.*

☐ *Your unsolved problems aren't worded in accordance with the guidelines, so the student doesn't understand what you're asking about or is becoming defensive.*

☐ *The student doesn't trust you yet, and is accustomed to having his concerns dismissed. Good that you're in this for the long haul.*

☐ *The student is convinced that he's in trouble or that you're just going to lower the boom once you get the information you're looking for. Multiple repetitions of Plan B—where his concerns are not only heard but also addressed—should help convince him otherwise.*

☐ *The student needs time to think about his concerns or needs help verbalizing them. Fortunately, we're not in a hurry.*

☐ *You're having trouble drilling for information. (Check the Drilling Cheat Sheet for help along these lines.)*

Question: When will I feel like I've mastered Plan B?

Answer: Every Plan B is different. Kids are different, and respond differently to Plan B. Unsolved problems are different. Some that seem relatively straightforward are more complex once you start drilling for information; others that seem complex turn out to be fairly straightforward. Some concerns are easier to talk about than others. Like all new skills, using Plan B becomes more instinctive with repeated practice. A few things you definitely want to avoid, though: leaving the Empathy step prematurely (better to overdrill than to underdrill); not being clear about your concerns in the Define Adult Concerns step; and agreeing on a solution that isn't realistic and mutually satisfactory. But if you're doing a good job of gathering information about the student's concerns, and doing well at entering your concerns into consideration, and working together with students to come up with realistic and mutually satisfactory solutions, you're certainly well on your way.

> *If you're doing a good job of gathering information about the student's concerns, and doing well at entering your concerns into consideration, and working together with students to come up with realistic and mutually satisfactory solutions, you're certainly well on your way.*

Question: This is not just a new way of thinking . . . it's a new way of talking, yes?

Answer: Yes. A lot of things that are said instinctively about and to behaviorally challenging students are changed when the CPS model is being implemented. Here are some examples.

OLD: *He's manipulative (or attention seeking or coercive or unmotivated or limit-testing).*

NEW: *He's lacking some very important skills, and has problems that have gone unsolved for a very long time.*

OLD: *We need to teach him who's the boss.*

NEW: *We need to identify those lagging skills, so we're seeing him through accurate lenses.*

OLD: *We need to apply consequences for those behaviors.*

NEW: *We need to identify and solve the problems that are causing those behaviors.*

OLD: *We can't let him get away with that behavior!*

NEW: *We are not letting him get away with anything. We're working on solving the problems that are causing that behavior.*

OLD: *He doesn't want to do well.*

NEW: *He's lacking the skills to do well.*

OLD: *He only does well when he wants to.*

NEW: *He does well when he has the skills to do well.*

The things we say to behaviorally challenging students change as well:

OLD: *Go to the office.*

NEW: *What's up?*

OLD: *You have a detention, young man.*

NEW: *When can we get together to solve this problem?*

EXPERIENCE IS THE BEST TEACHER

❝One of the indicators that tell me if I am having a successful Plan B session with a student is to think about who is doing most of the talking. The goal is for me to talk very little. At my best, I am asking key questions, summarizing what the student is telling me, proposing potential solutions, and, most important, demonstrating understanding and belief in the student. When I am able to focus on my role in this process, and the student is doing most of the talking, CPS has been much more successful.❞

—RYAN, ASSISTANT PRINCIPAL

❝When people are learning to use Plan B, sometimes they don't do it right the first time. They may skip a step, or they may slip back into Plan A. So sometimes you may not do it right, and you may slip back into your old patterns, but, eventually, with practice and with being aware and being reflective, you'll get it."

—NINA, PRINCIPAL

"The proactive part is crucial. You never process with a person who's out of control. That's when he's the least likely to be able to process what you're saying, and you're in his face and you're saying, 'You know your choices. Either calm down or you're going to lose recess.' That never works."

—ANONYMOUS, EDUCATIONAL TECHNICIAN

"Sometimes when the student isn't talking, it's because I'm not being proactive and I'm doing Emergency Plan B. One of the red flags for me is to realize this and admit, 'I'm doing Emergency Plan B here, and I have to reschedule this for a proactive time.' If you sit down with somebody and say, 'So tell me about how rude you're being' or 'Tell me about how you're hitting your classmates'—if you're focusing on behavior—then the conversation is negative from the beginning, and the child is not going to open up. And even five-year-olds, if they think they're in trouble, if they think we're talking about their behavior, they're going to shut down."

—NINA, PRINCIPAL

"If you can get the Empathy step right, then you take a huge step toward that goal of building teacher-student relationships. So if a classroom teacher can listen to a child's perspective—really listen and not just pay lip service—you're moving in the right direction. If you're not real, the kids know it. It's really important for us to consider feedback from adults who have been helped at some point along the way. The number one thing they tell us is that somebody cared about them—somebody listened. Someone was there for me. And they didn't judge me and they let me talk about it and work it out."

—TOM, ASSISTANT SUPERINTENDENT

CHAPTER 8

THE LOGISTICS

This chapter could have been placed much earlier in the book, as it describes the most challenging aspect of implementing the CPS model in a school: *organizing and sustaining the effort.* And you want to plan for this aspect before you begin trying to tackle everything else you've read about so far. But it seemed to make more sense to describe the CPS model in its entirety before getting to the really hard part. Now that you know what you're trying to accomplish, we can give more consideration to the nuts and bolts of making it happen.

Yes, it can be hard to learn to use the ALSUP, but not that hard. It just takes practice. And it can be challenging to master Plan B. But if you put in enough reps, self-assess how things go each time, get a handle on the routine pitfalls you seem to be falling into, guard against those pitfalls in each subsequent Plan B, and practice some more, you'll be fine. It'll start coming more naturally.

Organizing and sustaining the effort is much harder. So here are two important words to get you started: *start small.* Although it's very tempting to think that it will be possible to get everyone in the building good at the CPS model in one fell swoop, it's just not gonna happen. Until there's a cadre of staff in each building who are proficient in the model—until you've "built capacity," so to speak—it's unlikely that the model will be sustained. It'll just be another good idea that didn't stick. Better to plan ahead so that doesn't happen.

> *Until there's a cadre of staff in each building who are proficient in the model—until you've "built capacity," so to speak—it's unlikely that the model will be sustained.*

STEPS TO ORGANIZING AND SUSTAINING THE EFFORT

So let's think about the specific components that will get and keep the ball rolling.

Step 1: Select the Core Group

Although it's fine to do a book study on CPS for the entire staff, starting small means that after the book study is completed, the cadre of staff—usually seven or eight participants, often called the *core group*—who are going to become proficient in the model must first begin meeting regularly (preferably weekly) to ensure continuity of effort. The core group should expect to meet over a duration of approximately four to six months to achieve proficiency in the CPS model. Then—and not really before—they'll be ready to help others in the building become proficient in the model as well.

Who should be selected for the core group? Certainly, staff members willing to devote the time, resolve, and extra energy to practicing and mastering the key components of the CPS model. It might seem that the core group should comprise only staff members enthusiastic about the CPS model, but it's actually good strategy to include participants who are still on the fence or even philosophically opposed, especially if they're open minded and willing to give the model a good try. Early antipathy toward the model shouldn't be viewed as a permanent state of affairs; in all the schools, inpatient psychiatric units, residential facilities, and juvenile detention centers in which the CPS model has been implemented, many of those who were most resistant early on became among the most ardent advocates for the model over time.

The core group should also include staff with influence in the building; if they're excluded, there's the risk that they'll go "underground" and undermine the effort. And the core group should definitely include the principal and the assistant or vice principal. They need to get their hands dirty and their feet wet right alongside everyone else. More about school leaders in a later section.

Perhaps the most crucial characteristics of core group members are bravery, a willingness to make and discuss mistakes, and perseverance. Changing practices and being more responsive to behaviorally challenging students can feel daunting. Becoming proficient in using the ALSUP and Plan B requires fortitude.

Step 2: Get Comfortable with the ALSUP

The core group should not spend much time debating competing views and philosophies on behaviorally challenging kids, as such debates seldom reconcile anything. Better to just get started with the nuts and bolts of the CPS model. The first thing the core group should tackle is the ALSUP. Core group members should complete ASLUPs in real meetings with real staff about real students and bring those completed ALSUPs to core group meetings where members review and critique the wording of unsolved problems, with the guidelines as their reference point. Then they should do it again. And again. After three to five weeks, the core group members should be feeling a lot better about their skills in using the ALSUP.

Step 3: Practice Plan B—a Lot

Mastery of Plan B comes next. Core group members should practice Plan B with real students on real unsolved problems, and if the school allows, audio-record the discussions and play those recordings in core group meetings. Members should provide feedback to each other on each step, with the Drilling Cheat Sheet and Plan B Cheat Sheet (Figure 8.1) guiding the way. Then they should go back and do it again. And again. After twelve to fifteen weeks, members should be starting to feel pretty good about their Plan B skills.

To download the Plan B Cheat Sheet, go to www.livesinthebalance.org/LostandFound.

Step 4: Expand the Effort

After gaining proficiency with the ALSUP and Plan B, the core group members can begin strategizing about how to introduce colleagues to the model and create mechanisms for those colleagues to practice what they're learning. The colleagues probably already have familiarity with the ALSUP, because core group members have practiced using the ASLUP in meetings. To expose colleagues to Plan B, it's often helpful to have staff sit in as observers on Plan Bs being done by core group members. Although some people find role-playing Plan B to be useful, I often find role plays to be a bit contrived; when it comes to practice, there's nothing like the real thing. It's often thought that students will be uncomfortable with another adult observing the Plan B, but

Empathy Step

Ingredient/Goal:	Words:	More Help:	What You're Thinking:	Don't . . .
Gather information about and achieve a clear understanding of the kid's concern or perspective on the unsolved problem you're discussing.	**Initial Inquiry (neutral observation):** "I've noticed that [insert unsolved problem] . . . what's up?" **Drilling for Information:** Usually involves reflective listening and asking clarifying questions; gathering information related to the who, what, where, and when of the unsolved problem; and asking the kid what he or she is thinking in the midst of the unsolved problems and why the problem occurs under some conditions and not others.	If you're not sure what to say next, want more info, or are confused by something the kid has said, say: • "How so?" • "I'm confused." • "I don't quite understand." • "Can you tell me more about that?" • "Let me think about that for a second." If the kid doesn't talk or says "I don't know," try to figure out why: • Maybe the unsolved problem wasn't free of challenging behavior, wasn't specific, wasn't free of adult theories, or was "clumped" (instead of split). • Maybe you're using Emergency Plan B (instead of Proactive Plan B). • Maybe you're using Plan A. • Maybe the kid really doesn't know. • Maybe the kid needs the problem broken down into its component parts. Maybe the kid needs time to think.	"What don't I yet understand about the kid's concern or perspective? What doesn't make sense to me yet? What do I need to ask to understand it better?"	Skip the Empathy step Assume you already know what the kid's concern is and treat the Empathy step as if it were a formality Rush through the Empathy step Leave the Empathy step before you completely understand the kid's concern or perspective Talk about solutions yet

Define Adult Concerns Step

Ingredient/Goal:	Words:	More Help:	What You're Thinking:	Don't . . .
Enter the concern of the second party (often the adult) into consideration	"The thing is [insert adult concern]" or "My concern is [insert adult concern]"	Most adult concerns fall into one of two categories: How the problem is affecting the kid How the problem is affecting others	"Have I been clear about my concerns? Does the child understand what I have said?"	Start talking about solutions yet Sermonize, judge, lecture, or use sarcasm

Invitation Step

Ingredient/Goal:	Words:	More Help:	What You're Thinking:	Don't . . .
Brainstorm solutions that are realistic (meaning both parties can do what they are agreeing to) and mutually satisfactory (meaning the solution truly addresses the concerns of both parties)	Restate the concerns that were identified in the first two steps, usually beginning with "I wonder if there is a way . . ."	Stick as closely as possible to the concerns that were identified in the first two steps. While it's a good idea to give the kid the first opportunity to propose a solution, generating solutions is a team effort. It's a good idea to consider the odds of a given solution actually working. If you think the odds are below 60–70 percent, consider what it is that's making you skeptical and talk about it. This step always ends with agreement to return to Plan B if the first solution doesn't stand the test of time.	"Have I summarized both concerns accurately? Have we truly considered whether both parties can do what they've agreed to? Does the solution truly address the concerns of both parties? What's my estimate of the odds of this solution working?"	Rush through this step either Enter this step with preordained, "ingenious" solutions Sign off on solutions that both parties can't actually perform Sign off on solutions that don't truly address the concerns of both parties

Figure 8.1: Drilling Cheat Sheet and Plan B Cheat Sheet

I don't typically find that to be the case, though it's good to be sensitive to the possibility.

Next, Plan B novices should take the lead on a few Plan Bs, with a core group member sitting in to provide guidance, coaching, and feedback as needed. There are guidelines for such coaching and feedback later in this chapter. Over time, in the exact same way that core group members eventually became more confident and independent in their use of Plan B, the novices become more confident and independent as well. Then they aren't novices anymore.

Slowly but surely, staff start to experience success with the model. They have jaw-dropping moments in the Empathy step, moments when they discover that their notions about kids' concerns were inaccurate. They notice that kids are willing to listen to adult concerns, and even take them into account in generating solutions. Problems that have been causing challenging behavior for a very long time start getting solved. The ALSUP and Problem Solving Plan become integral components of meetings. The components of the model become routine. The lenses change. The language changes. The practices change. CPS becomes the norm; it becomes automatic. This doesn't happen fast, but it does happen.

> *Problems that have been causing challenging behavior for a very long time start getting solved. Slowly but surely, the model becomes the norm in the building.*

How long does it take? Well, it's going to take the core group four to six months to master the ALSUP and Plan B. Then it's going to take another year for everyone in the building to be exposed to the model and to get some supervised experience in using it. And then it's going to take one more year for the model to become the norm. If that sounds like a long time, consider what we're trying to accomplish here: *completely transforming the manner in which behaviorally challenging students are understood and treated.*

That's no small undertaking. It's worth it. Very few transformative changes in schools happen more quickly. It's the quick fixes that end up taking the longest time.

The reality is that each school has its own timing on accomplishing the mission. The schools that have had the greatest success with the CPS model didn't just "taste" the model as though they were sampling wines—they committed to *doing* it. Many even established specific goals, and time lines for achieving those goals. One thing is almost guaranteed: some staff members are going to struggle with and passively or actively resist the change. Some people find the tenets of the CPS model to be at odds with their own thinking or training. It's important to clarify whether there's actually much thinking behind the thinking. There are so many clichés applied to behaviorally challenging students (see chapter 2), and those clichés so often take on lives of their own, that initial reactions to the CPS model often aren't based on deep philosophical beliefs but rather those clichés. Gently challenging clichés can be productive.

Ultimately, the goal is for all staff members to move off of some of the automatic thoughts that kick in when they're dealing with challenging behavior (*She's doing this to make me mad/She's trying to get thrown out of my class/Her parents are incompetent disciplinarians/What consequences can I impose to teach her a lesson and let her know I take this behavior seriously?*) and replace them with more accurate, compassionate thoughts (*She's not challenging all the time, only some of the time/ What is her challenging behavior communicating about the expectations she's having difficulty meeting?/What are those expectations telling me about the skills she's lacking?/When am I going to do Plan B to solve those problems with her?*). There is tremendous harm being done by the first group of thoughts. Harm is what happens when helpers aren't helping.

THE ROLE OF ADMINISTRATORS

Now, one more essential word: *leadership*. Without question, the schools that have had the greatest success with CPS are those in which school leaders led the way. Administrators assembled and galvanized the core group. They were active participants in the core group; they were in the trenches, just like everyone else. They helped people keep their eyes on the ball. They celebrated successes; they empathized and were supportive when things were hard and didn't go so well. They expressed confidence that transforming discipline was something the school not only *could* accomplish but *had* to accomplish. They made sure that people stayed focused on the high stakes: the fates of our most vulnerable students and what we teach all of our students about how to deal with individual differences.

ENGAGE PARENTS

At some point along the way, you'll want to involve parents in the collaborative effort as well. I've seen some schools involve parents from the get-go; others wanted some time to get comfortable with the CPS model before involving parents. Either approach is OK; but if you choose to hold off, don't wait forever.

Over the years, a lot of the parents I've worked with have stated that they felt blamed and uninformed by their children's school; that they haven't felt listened to by school personnel; and that teachers and administrators were very keen on Plan A, not only in interactions with the kids but also in interactions with the parents. Amazingly enough, many teachers had some of the same complaints about the parents! What's clear is that Plan B is just as applicable to teacher-parent problem solving as it is to teacher-student problem solving.

> *What's clear is that Plan B is just as applicable to teacher-parent problem solving as it is to teacher-student problem solving.*

Here are a few statements of the obvious. Blaming is remarkably counterproductive, even if it seems clear that a student is going home to a situation that is less than ideal. And imposing your will on others (Plan A) is not the ideal path to fruitful collaboration and communication.

Yes, many kids who exhibit behavioral challenges at school are going home to problematic family circumstances. But many well-behaved kids come out of less-than-ideal situations too. And many behaviorally challenging kids come out of seemingly idyllic families. Yes, many kids who are behaviorally challenging at school are also behaviorally challenging at home, but that just means that the kid is struggling to meet expectations in multiple environments, and that the problems haven't yet been solved in those multiple environments. But that also means that the adults in those different environments have shared concerns and frustrations. And that should make collaborating easier, not harder.

Do the home folks need to be a party to every Plan B that takes place at school? No way. In fact, the home folks don't need to be involved in *most* of the Plan Bs that take place at school, because the unsolved problems don't involve them. Some unsolved problems at school do involve the parents—for example, truancy, tardiness, incomplete homework—but most do not. So while it's a very good idea to keep parents informed of the problems being solved at school, their actual involvement in Plan B is frequently unnecessary.

And what about circumstances in which efforts to collaborate with parents aren't going well? The very same pitfalls that apply to adult-child problem solving are equally applicable to adult-adult problem solving (see chapter 7). For example, using Plan A instead of Plan B. Using Emergency Plan B instead of Proactive Plan B. Failing to identify and clarify the concerns of both parties. Dueling solutions (power struggles) are a big one. If all else fails, never forget that you can still do a kid a lot of good in the six hours a day, five days a week, nine months a year that she's in school, even if her parents aren't involved in the effort. And that the kids who are going home to situations that aren't ideal need the folks at school to be on their game more than anyone else.

TEACHING COLLEAGUES ABOUT PLAN B

Teaching colleagues about using Plan B can be challenging. It's not easy to maintain a balance between providing colleagues with feedback, helping them maintain their optimism, and promoting independence. So here are some pointers on being a good teacher and coach.

Introduce the Plans and Plan B

First, novices need to know about the ALSUP and how it's used. But we covered that previously in the book, so let's assume that the novices are now ready to learn about the Plans and Plan B. Here are the key points to emphasize along these lines.

1. **Describe the three Plans in detail,** *beginning with Plan C.* Emphasize that Plan C is the *prioritizing* Plan. Be sure to make the distinction between prioritizing and "giving in" or "capitulating." Point out that prioritizing is important because it helps caregivers avoid trying to solve every unsolved problem in one fell swoop. It's best to indicate that Plan C involves *setting aside* unsolved problems rather than *dropping* them forever.

2. **Describe both Plan A and Plan B as** *attempts to solve the problem* that are distinguished primarily by the fact that Plan A is *unilateral* and involves the imposition of adult will (as denoted by the words *"I've decided that . . ."*) and (often) adult-imposed consequences, while Plan B is *collaborative* and involves a partnership between student and adult. Emphasize that solutions arrived at through use of Plan A are also *uninformed*, whereas solutions arrived at through Plan B are informed by the information gathered from the student in the Empathy step.

3. **In describing the three steps of Plan B, provide an example of what each step would sound like.** Best to use an unsolved problem that has been identified on the ALSUP that

has already been completed for a particular student. Providing an example also increases the likelihood that, when it comes time for people to observe Plan B, they'll recognize what they're seeing. Describe the Empathy step as the part of the problem-solving process where information is being gathered from the student about her concerns, perspective, or point of view on a given unsolved problem; the Define Adult Concerns step is where the caregiver enters his or her concern into consideration; and the Invitation is where student and adult collaborate on solutions that are realistic and mutually satisfactory.

4. **Indicate that the introduction to the Empathy step begins with the words** *"I've noticed that"* **and ends with the words** *"What's up?"* Inserted between these two stems is the unsolved problem. By the way, the best time to introduce the drilling strategies and the Drilling Cheat Sheet is when you're providing an example of what the Empathy step would sound like. If you don't describe the drilling strategies, the caregivers will have no idea what you're doing when they're observing Plan B.

5. **Indicate that the Define Adult Concerns step begins with the words** *"My concern is . . ."* **or** *"The thing is . . ."* Also point out that caregiver concerns almost always fall into one or both of two categories: how the unsolved problem is affecting the kid and/or how the unsolved problem is affecting other people. You'll want to reiterate that there's no discussion of solutions until the Invitation step.

6. **Emphasize that the Invitation step begins with the words** *"I wonder if there's a way . . ."* Although the kid is given the first crack at the solution (that's good strategy), coming up with solutions is a team effort.

7. **Gauge people's reactions to the three Plans.** Clarify points about which they may be confused, and facilitate a discussion about how Plan B differs from the ways in which they've been solving problems thus far.

8. **Make sure people are aware that Plans B and C are best used** *proactively*. If you provide examples of Plans B and C, make sure the examples are proactive so that people aren't confused about the timing. Remind colleagues that the hard work that was devoted to identifying unsolved problems on the ALSUP—and the prioritizing that occurs with the Problem Solving Plan—are what make proactive intervention possible.

> *Remind colleagues that the hard work that was devoted to identifying unsolved problems on the ALSUP—and the prioritizing that occurs with the Problem Solving Plan—are what make proactive intervention possible.*

Demonstrating Plan B

Telling people about Plan B is great, but *showing* them Plan B is indispensable. When core group members become confident in their use of Plan B, they're ready to start demonstrating its use to novices in the building. As you've read, this can occur in various formats. The core group member can do Plan B with one of his or her own students, with the novice—having already been introduced to the three Plans and to the three steps of Plan B—sitting in to observe. Or the core group member can do Plan B with one of the novice's students, with the novice pitching in (especially in the Define Adult Concerns and Invitation steps). To help novices get the most out of the Plan Bs they observe, it's productive for the demonstrator to actually *describe* what he or she is doing at each step along the way. This can feel very strange to the demonstrator; but observers appreciate the connections that are made between what they've previously been told about Plan B and what they're now seeing in action.

Here are some guidelines for what to say for each of the steps:

Narrate the wording of the introduction: "You may remember that the introduction begins with the words, 'I've noticed that . . .' and ends with the words 'What's up?' In between, I'll insert the unsolved problem we decided we'd be talking about with Joelle today. So here goes: *Joelle, I've noticed that it's been difficult for you to write the three paragraphs on Hermann Hesse's* Siddhartha *. . . what's up?*"

Narrate the drilling strategies: "OK, Joelle's response was that it's boring. So, as you know, the first thing the kid says doesn't usually give us a very clear sense of her concern, perspective, or point of view on the unsolved problem, so now it's time for me to start drilling for more information. And I'm going to be using the drilling strategies on the Drilling Cheat Sheet that you have in front of you. The one that makes the most sense to me right now is reflective listening, which is where I'm simply saying back to Joelle what she just said to me and clarifying further. So here goes: *So, it's boring. Can you tell me more about that?*"

Continue narrating the drilling strategies: It's very easy to get "caught up doing Plan B" and forget to tell the observer what you're doing. But what you're doing will make more sense to him if you're actually telling him.

Let the observer know when you're summarizing: "OK, so we've gathered a fair amount of information from Joelle on this problem. Let me summarize what we've heard so far and ask Joelle if she has any other concerns to share."

Let the observer know when you're leaving the Empathy step and moving on to the Define Adult Concerns step: "OK, so Joelle has told me that she has no other concerns to tell me about on this unsolved problem. So now I'm going to move on to the Define Adult Concerns step. This is where I'm going to tell her my concern, and that usually begins with the words, 'The thing is . . .' or 'My concern is . . .' So here we go:

Joelle, my concern is that if you don't write the three paragraphs on Siddhartha, *I'm not going to know if you read it and understood the material."*

Let the observer know when you're leaving the Define Adult Concerns step and moving on to the Invitation step: "OK, so now I've told Joelle my concerns. So next we'll move on to the Invitation. Notice, we haven't started discussing solutions yet because we had to make sure we understood the concerns of both parties first. But now we're ready. The Invitation begins with the words, 'I wonder if there's a way . . .' And what I'm going to try to do here is recap or restate the concerns we heard about in those first two steps. Ready? *So, Joelle, I wonder if there's something we can do about the fact that you're having a very hard time understanding what information I'm looking for in the three paragraphs . . . and a very hard time understanding* Siddhartha *in the first place . . . and I can know if you've read and understood the material.* And now I'm going to give Joelle the first crack at the solution; again, not because it's her job to solve the problem, but because I want her to know that I'm very interested in her ideas. So now I say to Joelle, *Do you have any ideas?"*

Narrate the processing of solutions: "All right, Joelle has suggested that maybe I could help her understand *Siddhartha* and clarify what I'm looking for in the three paragraphs after school one day. Now we need to figure out if that meets our two criteria for good solutions: they need to be realistic and mutually satisfactory. Let's do mutually satisfactory first. That's where we consider whether the solution would address the concerns of both parties. Let's think about those concerns again. I think it would address Joelle's concern that she needs help understanding *Siddhartha* and my expectations for the three paragraphs. *Joelle, do you agree?* And it would address my concern that I want to know that Joelle's reading and understanding the book. But I'm wondering about the mutually satisfactory part. *Joelle, are you sure you're able to stay after school? I know you take the school bus, and that makes staying after hard for you."*

Agree to return to Plan B if the first solution doesn't get the job done: "So, it sounds like we're ready to run with the solution. I'm now going to remind Joelle that if the first solution doesn't work, we'll get together again, figure out why, and come up with a different solution."

Do kids mind all that narrating? No, they're often interested in what's going on. Is narrating hard for the demonstrator? Yes. Does it make it easier for the observer to understand what's going on in preparation for his first attempt at Plan B? No question.

> *Is narrating hard for the demonstrator? Yes. Does it make it easier for the observer to understand what's going on in preparation for his first attempt at Plan B? No question.*

Coaching Plan B

Let's now think more about the two most important words to characterize your efforts to coach others in the use of Plan B: *promote independence*. Your goal as a coach is to help Plan B apprentices become increasingly independent in using Plan B, and the nature of the feedback you provide will be crucial in this regard. In other words, there's feedback and coaching that promote greater and lesser levels of independence. You don't want the apprentice to twist in the winds of Plan B, but you do want to provide feedback that promotes as much independence as the apprentice can handle.

The least independence-promoting form of coaching is to simply *take the reins* of Plan B if the apprentice is struggling (for example, *"OK, I'm going to take over here"*). Although this might be necessary in some instances—just to make sure that the Plan B goes well or to keep both parties hanging in there—it's not an especially independence-promoting approach. Somewhat more independence promoting is to *tell the apprentice exactly what to say or do* (for example, *"You need to do reflective listening here . . . say back to Joelle what she just said to you"*). This may also be necessary sometimes, especially with apprentices who are brand new to Plan B, but it's still not going to promote much independence. Still more independence promoting is to provide more general guidance or reminders, but without explicitly telling the apprentice what to say or do (for example, *"You may want to think about whether you're really ready to leave the Empathy step just yet"* or *"Don't forget the two categories of adult concerns"* or *"You may want to think about the concerns of both parties before you sign off on that solution"* or *"I don't know if you're going to be able to address all those concerns in one Plan B"*). The most independence-promoting strategy, of course, is to say virtually nothing while the apprentice is doing Plan B (assuming it's going well). This is a sign that you've been a very good coach and that the apprentice is no longer an apprentice.

Q & A

Question: In schools that have implemented CPS, where did they find the time to do it?

Answer: Time is the factor that impedes all new initiatives in schools. So every building has to deal with the time issue in implementing CPS. Now, as you've read, Plan B can be done during some existing blocks of time during the course of a school day: before school, after school, during lunch or recess or the teacher's prep time (if the teacher has prep time). One of the reasons it's so important to have building leaders integrally involved in the implementation process is that they're often in a position to create time, whether by providing coverage or rearranging schedules. But the key factor here is commitment to making the time. If time is left to random chance, there won't be much Plan B going on nor many problems being solved.

So, many schools have implemented something called 15 Minutes a Day. This involves every teacher in the building committing to carving out fifteen minutes every day to solving problems with individual kids. That's seventy-five minutes a week. Five hours a month. Forty-five hours every school year that every teacher in the building is committing to solving problems with kids. Best to start with the behaviorally challenging ones, the ones causing the most disruption to their own learning and that of others. If you're systematic and diligent about it, you're going to get a lot of problems solved with those kids over the course of the first three to four months. Then it's time to turn to the others.

By the way, the others have probably noticed what you're doing. I had an elementary school teacher tell me that after three to four months of doing 15 Minutes a Day, one of her well-behaved students approached her and asked if he could have one of those slots, as he had something he wanted to talk with her about. She was both amused and eager to hear what he had to say.

Question: Who should do Plan B with a given student on a particular problem?

Answer: Early on, it will presumably be a member of the core group, as core group members are the only staff dedicating time and practice to becoming proficient in the model. But, as you've read, once that happens, core group members start inviting other staff to sit in on and observe Plan Bs so that those other staff have a feel for the process. Then those staff start trying to lead Plan B discussions with a core group member sitting in, to provide coaching and feedback. Then, just as the core group members did, those staff start trying Plan B independently.

Eventually, the ideal person to do Plan B with a student is the staff member whose expectation the student is having difficulty meeting. What if the relationship between that student and staff member is so far gone that Plan B feels impossible? Have someone else—someone the student is most likely to talk to—lead the Plan B, perhaps with the staff member sitting in as well. If things go as hoped, eventually the staff member and student will be able to do Plan B together without facilitation by someone else.

> *The ideal person to do Plan B with a student is the staff member whose expectation the student is having difficulty meeting.*

Question: There are a lot of initiatives for behaviorally challenging kids in schools these days. Which ones are most compatible with the CPS model?

Answer: Here's the interesting thing about all those initiatives: they're often implemented in very different ways in different schools and school systems. An initiative that is transformative in one school or school system barely changes mentalities and practices in another. So a lot of the compatibility with CPS depends on where the school or school system is in its journey to a more compassionate, enlightened view of kids' behavioral challenges.

But let's take 'em one at a time. There is significant congruence between the goals, structure, and practices of Response to Intervention (RTI) and the CPS model. For the unfamiliar, the impetus for RTI comes, at least partially, from the recognition that the needs of many students receiving services in special education could be met in general education classrooms. Thus the first and most important school personnel to implement intervention are classroom teachers. The CPS model is an excellent fit with RTI in this regard. RTI also represents an attempt to introduce scientific, data-based methods into school classrooms to guide the selection, use, and evaluation of academic and behavioral interventions. CPS is a good fit along these lines as well.

There's also some congruence between CPS and Positive Behavioral Interventions and Supports (PBIS), but some significant points of divergence as well. The two models are certainly similar in their emphasis on proactive, preventive intervention and in the belief that children with challenging behavior should be treated with the same level of interest and importance as children with academic challenges. However, in assessing the function of a kid's challenging behavior, PBIS is still largely oriented toward viewing the behavior as "working" for a kid by helping her get, escape, and avoid. As you know, this contrasts with the view in CPS that behavior is simply the mechanism by which a student communicates that she is lacking the skills to respond adaptively to certain expectations. Thus, while PBIS allows for the possibility of lagging skills as an explanation for challenging behavior, it places a strong emphasis on using environmental reinforcement to train replacement behaviors. The CPS model places a strong emphasis on adult-child problem solving as the primary mechanism for teaching lagging thinking skills and helping kids solve problems. But perhaps the most striking difference between the two models is that PBIS doesn't involve collaboration between adult and kid; it is an adult-driven model. There is no major emphasis on collaborating with kids to identify their concerns (only a major emphasis on identifying *adult* concerns) and no emphasis on enlisting the kid in coming up with a mutually satisfactory action plan; rather, the *adults* come up with the action plan.

In many ways, CPS is also philosophically aligned with Restorative Justice (RJ) and restorative practices. Both CPS and RJ eschew traditional, punitive disciplinary procedures. Both place a strong emphasis on relationships and community building. RJ posits that "harmers" will choose more adaptive options when they come to understand, through dialogue and conversation with those harmed, the pain they have caused by their misbehavior. The CPS model asserts that challenging kids will evidence more adaptive behavior when the problems precipitating challenging behavior and conflict are solved. Although various aspects of RJ can be viewed as reactive, there are a wide array of restorative practices that are more oriented toward conflict prevention, including problem-solving circles, which are a great addition to the model.

There is substantial overlap philosophically between CPS and Marshall Rosenberg's Nonviolent Communication (NVC) model, with some nuanced differences. The NVC paradigm places a heavy emphasis on empathy, clarifying concerns and feelings, and ways in which people communicate with one another that interfere with empathy and compassion. Although the precepts of NVC and CPS are congruent, CPS places a significantly stronger emphasis on lagging cognitive skills as the crucial factor contributing to challenging behavior.

Thomas Gordon's Teacher Effectiveness Training model shares many important themes with CPS as well, again without the emphasis on lagging cognitive skills and unsolved problems.

There are also crisis management models that overlap to some degree with the CPS model. But CPS isn't best thought of as a crisis management program. Crisis management programs are aptly named, as they're oriented toward *managing* crises. While it's good to know how to defuse and de-escalate a crisis—and Emergency Plan B is useful along these lines—CPS places significantly greater emphasis on crisis *prevention*. No other learning disability is handled in crisis mode, and a crisis is clearly not the best time to address the lagging skills and unsolved problems underlying social, emotional, and behavioral challenges.

Question: Is CPS truly realistic in a middle, junior, or senior high school, where kids have multiple teachers who don't always have a chance to communicate with one another?

Answer: Many middle and high schools are organized in teams or learning communities, which makes collaboration and communication easier. Nothing takes the place of ensuring that staff members have the time to talk about high-priority kids and meet periodically (preferably, at least weekly) to monitor the kids' progress and modify the Problem Solving Plan. Again, the only models of care that don't require good communication are the ineffective ones.

> *The only models of care that don't require good communication are the ineffective ones.*

Question: I'm a school principal. I've been trying to help my teachers use CPS, and it's gone pretty well. But I have a few teachers who just aren't doing it. Advice?

Answer: Try to figure out why, starting with the Empathy step, as in *"I've noticed that you haven't been participating much in our CPS work. What's up?"* They may not be convinced about the rationale for Plan B. They may feel they don't have the skills to do Plan B yet. They may feel completely overwhelmed. They may be retiring soon and just don't see the point. They may have a bad case of Initiative Fatigue. We won't really know what their concerns are unless we ask. Then we can work toward ensuring that their concerns—and yours—are addressed. If CPS becomes the expectation for how teachers will handle unmet expectations in their classrooms, then we want to make sure those teachers get as much support as they need.

Question: How do you incorporate CPS into an IEP?

Answer: If you've identified a kid's lagging skills and unsolved problems (through use of the ALSUP) and established a set of priorities (through use of the Problem Solving Plan), you're ready to incorporate those priorities into an IEP. You're also ready to document how Plan B will be used to address those lagging skills and problems. You can find an example of an IEP that incorporates the language of CPS at www.livesinthebalance.org /LostandFound. And you'll find an example of a 504 Plan that incorporates the language of CPS in the same place.

Question: I'd like to incorporate CPS into my FBAs and Behavior Intervention Plans . . . are there examples of those as well?

Answer: Sure thing. You can find examples at www .livesinthebalance.org/LostandFound.

Question: How can we tell if our school is making progress in our handling of behaviorally challenging kids?

Answer: There's no single benchmark signifying that you've "arrived," given that improvement is an ongoing process. But there are some pretty clear indicators:

☐ The mentality toward challenging kids in your school is oriented toward lagging skills and unsolved problems, and people are routinely using the ALSUP in their assessment of these kids and the Problem Solving Plan in monitoring their progress.
☐ Staff members are skilled in and actively using Plan B.
☐ Structures supporting the use of CPS are in place, including mechanisms for (1) responding to behavior problems proactively rather than emergently; (2) communicating and collaborating across staff and with parents; (3) practicing, coaching, and monitoring Plan B skills; and (4) orienting new staff to the model.
☐ Mechanisms are in place for the continuous evaluation of school discipline, and discipline referrals, detentions, suspensions, and expulsions are dramatically declining. Many schools that have implemented the CPS model have seen reductions of as high as 80 percent in their use of discipline referrals, suspensions, and detentions.

EXPERIENCE IS THE BEST TEACHER

❝The core group is where people start talking about the model and how to utilize it. It's the nucleus for everything to grow from. It can be hard, because it's volunteer and it's often after school. But it's always nice to get some of those on-the-fence people to have some successes; they have a lot of credibility when they tell their colleagues, 'I tried this CPS thing the other day, and the problem actually got solved.' And when they say it, their colleagues are like, 'Oh really. So what's up with that? How can I get some of that?'"

—TOM, ASSISTANT SUPERINTENDENT

"Starting small is crucial. You can't come in schoolwide to start with. It's too big. And CPS is quite a drastic change from a lot of practices that happen in schools. So starting small, finding a key core team to start with, and really dedicating some time for them to show that CPS is a priority—all very important."

—CAROL, PRINCIPAL

"With the core group, you have people behind you who support you and remind you that you're doing the right thing. That's really important. Because some people are telling you you're being weak, you're not teaching the kids the right thing to do. You really need that supportive group, other people who are feeling the same way and learning along with you."

—KATIE, LEARNING CENTER TEACHER

"One of the important things to remember is that meaningful change takes time. Changing your school philosophy and culture around student motivation and behavior is incredibly meaningful. Be thoughtful, proactive, and patient. To facilitate this, building 'leadership density' at your school in the model is crucial. All the contemporary research on educational change models supports the notion that when schools build systems that allow for teacher/staff leadership and greater ownership of initiatives, then the capacity for growth and sustainability of that initiative is far more optimal over time. This approach was a key component in the success we had implementing CPS at our school."

—RYAN, ASSISTANT PRINCIPAL

"A lot of people in education have really big hearts, but they don't ask for help; they do things solo. They put so many things on their own plate that they feel very overwhelmed. You have to ask for help. That's what the core group is for. You have to have a buddy teacher to say, 'Hey, I really need to talk to this kid. Will you just keep an eye on my class while they're doing their silent reading?'"

—VICKI, DIRECTOR OF COMMUNICATIONS

❝❝Teaching the model to others can be the most challenging task. I think it is important to remember that 'people do well if they can' just like the kids. This is such a foreign concept for some teachers and staff that it is important to be 'assumption free' with them, just as you are with the students.❞❞

—RYAN, ASSISTANT PRINCIPAL

❝❝We would have a teacher bring a recording of a Plan B conversation to a core group meeting so they could receive feedback from the other members. That really shows that the culture is super healthy, that the person has courage, she trusts her colleagues. So there's that subtle piece of first getting people to put themselves out there to get the feedback. But then there's the next piece of getting the feedback that could help the person grow, where the real risk-taking happens.❞❞

—TOM, ASSISTANT SUPERINTENDENT

❝❝We have to value teachers' time, value what they do in the classroom, and allow them to understand that this is value added for them. When we were doing Plan B with a child, we would free up two or three other teachers to observe. So they could see that we made mistakes as we went through and that it was OK to make those mistakes, and we were all learning at the same time. It's important to give people the opportunity to see it in action before they try it themselves.❞❞

—SUSAN, PRINCIPAL

❝❝I think that a lot of people understand that we need to listen to kids and we need to ask them what is going on for them. I don't think there's any educator out there who would say, 'You know, I wish I knew a little less about my kids. I don't really want to know what's going on under the surface there.' Right? There's no one who says that.❞❞

—CAROL, PRINCIPAL

❝❝Plan B has really made a huge impact on our students, but it also affected our thought processes, the language we used, and the way we interacted with students. It was pretty life changing for all of us. I've been in other buildings, and I've seen teachers demand that a principal send a kid home for misbehaving. And then the principal is on the phone with the parents telling them they have to come pick up their kid. And it's like, oh my gosh, why? What will that accomplish?"

—KATHY, TEACHER

"In our building, the office is no longer the place where kids go for discipline. It's a place where a kid goes if she needs a hug, if she needs some space. So kids feel like it's a safe place."

—KATIE, LEARNING CENTER TEACHER

"For change to occur, you have to move beyond what people are going to think of what you're trying to do and stay true to your heart and self."

—VICKI, DIRECTOR OF COMMUNICATIONS

"As we were moving toward being more of a problem-solving school, I remember worrying that people were wondering why I'm letting my students get away with things. But what everybody else is thinking doesn't matter because you're doing what you know is going to work and what's right for this child."

—KATIE, LEARNING CENTER TEACHER

"It's a language now in our building. The kids know we're actually going to discuss the situation, and listen to what they have to say. We're going to bring up our concerns. You're going to tell your concerns. We're going to try to come up with a solution that addresses everyone's concerns."

—KATHY, TEACHER

"You're letting kids know they're an important part of the team."

—KATIE, LEARNING CENTER TEACHER

"Seeing kids who were doing poorly starting to do well is very convincing to teachers who are digging in their heels a little bit about CPS. When they see the kid starting to do well, they say, 'OK, this really does work.' And then they start trying it with the kids in their classroom.

We get that it takes time. It's not a week or a month. Literally, it is this ongoing work that in some cases, with some kids, can be years. And in the long run, it pays off. And those are the kids too that remember; they come back. They're the ones who have got you in the death grip hug when they see you again. They know on some level . . . they might not be able to verbalize it . . . what a difference it made in their lives.

I think that's why we all do what we do. I think because we love kids, we believe in kids, we want kids to do well. So when I think about that, I know there's nothing better than to be able to work with kids and make a difference. But it's a team effort. It's not just us. It's the parents. It's the teacher before. So I just feel lucky, lucky to be in a job where we get to be able to do that." "

—KATHY, TEACHER

"If you have success with a student and it's helpful and you're sharing that with other people, it builds an organic, grass-roots culture in the school that it's about us helping the kids, and it feeds the fire of, 'This works.' So when that happens, it builds on itself. I think it's really important for those people who are using it to share their successes with others in a genuine, excited way. We had one teacher voice-record her Plan B conversation on an iPhone and then play it back to staff in a staff meeting. And we all talked about what went well and what she would like to do differently in the future. And that kind of sharing helps everyone feel safe to try Plan B, which is half the battle." "

—TOM, ASSISTANT SUPERINTENDENT

"I can remember one particular teacher who, at times, would butt heads with students. This teacher had high expectations and truly cared about students, but would often find herself in a standoff with a particular student. The teacher and I sat down with the student so I could model a Plan B session with them. Afterwards, in debriefing with the teacher, her first comment was that she could not believe 'how much the kid talked,' and she said, 'I have a completely different view of him now.' She also shared that, even after some training with the model, she still felt that she wasn't confident in what to do. This experience had really helped her learn how to apply the structure of the model in a specific and meaningful way with a student. This teacher, who could have been a 'saboteur' to the process at our school, became one of our big advocates of the CPS model." "

—RYAN, ASSISTANT PRINCIPAL

"Open communication and celebrating the successes in an open forum are so important because I feel like when kids aren't doing well, it's kind of more public, but a lot of the successes are more private and behind closed doors.

I think staff get worried about doing the ALSUP and Plan B incorrectly, especially when they're starting off. So the core group is really important." "

—NINA, PRINCIPAL

" "To keep the implementation on an awareness level, it is so important to celebrate success. We had members of the implementation team share a CPS success story each month at staff meetings. It was just a few minutes of time, but it stated to the whole school that this initiative is important; it is a priority, and it is working for our students." "

—RYAN, ASSISTANT PRINCIPAL

" "We've also worked really hard to team with parents, and at showing them respect and empathy. I mean, we're often aware of their home life. But there's no judgment. Parents do well if they can, too. Certainly if it was unsafe, we would do what we're mandated to do. But we've seen how parents change and become partners with us. I think teachers sometimes forget how uncomfortable coming to school is for a lot of parents . . . especially the kind of parents whose homes don't fit the standard definition of ideal. We have a lot of transient families, and if we lowered the hammer on them, they'd move away. They would just go to another school. They would disappear." "

—KATHY, TEACHER

" "When I was a principal, I was often put in a position where I felt like I had to be a bad guy with the parents. And I can remember feeling so uncomfortable that parents thought I was angry with them or that it was their fault. But once you start partnering with them . . . now I can see them anywhere, and they're happy to see me, and when I say, 'How is your child doing?' they're so open about it. It's not an adversarial relationship." "

—VICKI, DIRECTOR OF COMMUNICATIONS

" "We had parents who would not even come in the building or would sit and talk with their head down and have no idea of what to say and refuse services. I remember a mom who never came to any school activities, never would come to parent-teacher conferences, nothing. And later I found out that it was because she felt we were blaming her. Kids don't want to be singled out. They don't want to behave badly. But you can look at their parents the same way. This mother wants to be a good mother. She doesn't want to feel uncomfortable coming to school. Now she's coming to parent-teacher conferences. I speak to her on a regular basis. We text each other. She'll text me in the morning and say, 'Hey, just to let you know . . . we had a rough morning.' And this was something that would never have happened if we hadn't been able to build a relationship with the families. I think it goes hand in hand, I really do. You're not just building relationships with students; you're also trying to build relationships with their parents. It's good when parents begin to see their child making strides at school . . . but what really hooks them is becoming part of the team.

It's a really cool thing, too, because I've had families in the last couple of years even come to our school and say, 'Hey, I heard that your school does these cool things with kids. I heard that you don't send kids home.' You know, when people say that, it starts the relationship off on that positive note because they've been to these other schools that keep suspending the kids and kicking them out. One child enrolled here who had been kicked out of four day cares. And we were like, 'Come on in. We'll help you.' And some parents are actually hearing about us from other towns now. Parents who feel so judged and shamed a lot of times are hearing that this is a No Judgment Zone that helps their child.

We have parents who we haven't yet been able to bring on board. They're just not there yet. They're not ready to connect with the school yet to make that relationship with us. But we're still working with their kid. And when the kids come to school and tell us some of the unpleasant things that have gone on at home, we support them.

One of our kids came to school saying she'd had a hard morning, and we learned that her mother had called her 'retarded' that morning. And I said, 'You know, your mother should not have said that to you. We say a lot of things when we're angry that we don't mean. And it's not OK. She shouldn't have said that, and you're not retarded.' So those parents aren't yet on board. But their daughter feels very supported at school. She is flourishing this year. She comes to us when there's a problem that needs to be solved.**"**

—Kathy, Teacher

"In our building, we were able to create a space that we turned into the problem-solving center. We call it the learning center. And we placed in the room one of our gifted education techs who has been using the model for about two or three years and has a wonderful way with children. That's her space, and she works with all the children. So any teacher who feels that a child needs to access that space can meet with the learning center teacher to do an ALSUP and create a plan, and the children can do problem solving with the teacher of the learning center or with a classroom teacher. And it's a very soothing environment. Some kids and teachers access the learning center a lot; others less so. But it's a place where they have lots of Plan B going on. It's been very successful. At first, some people thought that the learning center is where kids who act up go to play. So people were thinking, 'Well, they're being reinforced for their negative behavior, because they're choosing to act out to be able to go and play.' And that was not the case at all. It was a misperception.*"*

—NINA, PRINCIPAL

*"*It takes time to change people's mind-sets, depending on their existing beliefs. When some people learn about CPS, it clicks right away because their heart's aligned with it. But there are a lot of people whose mind-set isn't there, whether it's because of tradition, their own experiences, or whatever. They are in one belief system that says the reward-and-punishment model is going to be effective; you've just got to keep doing it harder and bigger to make it work. So hearing about a different model doesn't click with them. They need to see it; they need to experience it before they're going to be able to make a change. It can take a long time to change that mind-set. And in some places, just the fear of change can be pretty big.*"*

—CAROL, PRINCIPAL

*"*It takes a lot to create change. And I think it does make people nervous when it's something that they don't feel completely comfortable or knowledgeable in. So it takes that time to really understand CPS and change our mind-set and change the way we approach children or see children with challenging behaviors. I also think sometimes that outside influences don't always match the model. I'm talking about both societal and school-system pressure. There's a lot of common practice with the reward-and-punishment model. So I think you have to be grounded in your knowledge of the right way to approach children.*"*

—NINA, PRINCIPAL

*"*The best way to get change to happen is to have a few people doing something really well and getting results with it, because the word spreads organically throughout the organization quite quickly when things are moving forward. That piques interest, and when interest comes from within,

you're dealing with intrinsic motivation instead of external expectations or pressure.**"**

—Tom, ASSISTANT SUPERINTENDENT

"We've got new curriculum rolling out, and we've got innovation initiatives and changes to the way that we help students learn. And yeah, it's hard to maintain focus on something regardless of how strong we believe in it, because you're simply flooded with workshops to go to, initiatives to work with, and assessment and planning. It can really muddy the waters, and as tightly as you're trying to steer the ship in a direction, there are winds that'll push you off course.**"**

—Carol, PRINCIPAL

"When we decided to implement CPS in our schools, we agreed that administrators would be trained along with counseling staff and classroom teachers. We work in a large system and staff are mandated to go to trainings and they come back and do the same thing that they had been doing before. These are good, caring people, but between severely needy students and a system that grinds out new initiatives like flour, there is no way they can separate the wheat from the chaff. By going through the training alongside my staff, I separated CPS from all of the other initiatives that they had to deal with. By letting them see me struggle with the ALSUP and Plan B, I made a clear statement that we were all going to be learners and really move in a new direction.**"**

—Anonymous school principal

"There are many different initiatives out there, and it can be challenging to sift through them all, as there are times that they compete with one another. It is important to know that many of these initiatives can work together. In our school, elements of PBIS, Responsive Classroom, Restorative Justice, and CPS all live and breathe together in a specific and strategic way. The universal teaching and proactive nature of PBIS and Responsive Classroom, combined with the student voice and ownership of CPS, allow for a classroom culture that values explicit instruction and caring intervention practices at all RTI levels for students. This "recipe" resulted in a 50 percent reduction in office discipline referrals over a three-year period at our school. The driving force, or philosophy, behind it all was *kids do well if they can.***"**

—Ryan, ASSISTANT PRINCIPAL

CHAPTER 9

THE OTHERS

Most of what you've been reading in the prior eight chapters has been specific to behaviorally challenging kids. But, of course, they're not the only students in your building or classroom. What about the rest of 'em? Is the goal to have two different discipline programs in the building, one for the behaviorally challenging kids and one for everyone else? Why would you want to reserve Plan B for the behaviorally challenging kids? Don't the well-behaved students have problems that need to be solved as well?

No, it's not the goal to have two different discipline programs in the building. As you know, you don't need your traditional discipline program for the well-behaved kids, because the traditional discipline program isn't why they're behaving themselves in the first place. Yes, you want to be using Plan B with well-behaved kids too, because no matter how well behaved they are, at some point they'll have difficulty meeting certain expectations. If, as recommended in chapter 8, you get Plan B rolling with the behaviorally challenging, disruptive kids early on, you'll find that you start to have more time to solve problems with everyone. Everyone gets help meeting social, academic, and behavioral expectations.

But understanding, and helping students surmount, the factors that are making it hard for them to meet certain expectations isn't the only reason you want to use Plan B with everyone; *you also want to foster qualities on the more positive side of human nature.* Qualities that help kids treat each other kindly and with mutual respect. Qualities like empathy, appreciating how one's behavior is affecting others, taking another's perspective, honesty, and resolving disagreements in ways that do not involve conflict. It is when these skills are present that kids and other human beings display sensitivity, acceptance of individual differences, compassion, and cooperation. And it's when these skills are absent that the more noxious side of human nature—insensitivity, conflict, aggression, and destruction—rears its head.

Are the ways in which we're disciplining, teaching, and interacting with our students—and solving the problems that affect their lives—fostering those positive qualities? Regrettably, in far too many places and instances, the answer is no.

Research has shown that today's college students score 40 percent lower than their predecessors in their ability to understand what another person is feeling, and that the median narcissism score has risen 30 percent in two decades. How can this be, in an age in which so many schools are implementing community-building programs and emphasizing social and emotional learning? What are we doing wrong?

We're still doing way too much Plan A, and Plan A begets Plan A.

> *When we tell teachers to prioritize high-stakes testing and achievement—to the neglect of the skills that help humans display the more positive side of human nature—we do ourselves and future generations an enormous disservice.*

As you read in chapter 2, teachers have historically been among the most important agents of socialization in society. When we tell teachers to prioritize high-stakes testing and achievement—to the neglect of the skills that help humans display the more positive side of human nature—we do ourselves and future generations an enormous disservice. When we use power to solve problems with our kids, we teach our kids to use power to solve problems.

The reality is that we all want our concerns to be heard and validated. And we all want our concerns to be addressed. People—kids included—become marginalized, disenfranchised, alienated, and increasingly prone to hopelessness and sometimes violence when those two things don't happen.

In some schools—especially those where staff are cognizant of the reality that preparing kids for high-stakes tests is actually very poor preparation for the demands of the workplace in The Real World—there's been a movement toward the teaching of what are called "soft skills," including critical thinking, perseverance, the ability to collaborate, and the ability to benefit from feedback. The instruction in these schools is more project based and student centered, as opposed to the mere teaching of factual information. But we need to go further. Besides project-based and student-centered learning and community building, what additional technology is needed?

Well, you've been reading about it in this book. We know how to ensure that kids' concerns are heard, clarified, validated, and addressed, and that solutions are mutually satisfactory. That same technology helps us teach, practice, and display the characteristics on the more positive side of human nature.

Let's consider how more explicitly.

SKILLS FOSTERED THROUGH USE OF PLAN B

The first step of Plan B—the Empathy step—helps students practice thinking about and clarifying their concerns. It also helps them articulate concerns in a way that increases the likelihood that those concerns will be taken into account and addressed. What a crucial life skill! So often, we human beings—kids included—exhibit our least desirable traits when we have a concern and can't articulate what it is. Sometimes that's because we're convinced our concerns won't be heard, as the person we're interacting with isn't giving us the chance to voice them. Sometimes it's because the emotions associated with the concerns have flooded in too quickly, so we end up expressing powerful emotions rather than the concerns driving those emotions. And sometimes we react in mere anticipation of a battle. The Empathy step slows things down for everyone, and helps ensure that we're focused on the right currency: concerns, not power.

What do students learn in the Empathy step? They learn that their concerns are valid and will be heard and addressed rather than being dismissed, disparaged, or belittled. What do adults learn in the Empathy step? They learn how to empathize and take another person's concerns into account. Why are teachers frequently so surprised to learn their students' real concerns? Often because they've never heard those concerns . . . sometimes because they've never really asked. Kids whose concerns are heard and taken into account are far more receptive to listening to and taking into account the concerns of others.

A student's ability to communicate about his concerns is vital, since concerns are the currency of Plan B and since durable, mutually satisfactory solutions must address the concerns of both parties. But that ability is important not only for participating in Plan B; it's important in life.

> *The ability to communicate one's concerns is important not only for participating in Plan B; it's important in life.*

There are many young people in the world—I've worked with some of them in prisons and residential facilities—who have been on the receiving end of society's most punitive interventions for a very long time. Many of them have given up on being heard and understood. But they still recognize when someone's listening, taking their concerns seriously, and working to ensure that those concerns are addressed. That's when we start to see that they still have the capacity for the better side of human nature.

> *Students learn and practice many skills in the Define Adult Concerns step . . . empathy, taking into account another person's perspective, and appreciating how one's behavior is affecting others. These are . . . among the most important skills in the human repertoire.*

Students learn and practice many skills in the Define Adult Concerns step as well, including empathy, taking into account another person's perspective, and appreciating how one's behavior is affecting others. These are, without question, among the most important skills in the human repertoire. They play a huge role in helping us treat each other with compassion and sensitivity. They help us refrain from conduct that is harmful to others. While rules and laws and enforcement are wonderful, these are external controls, and they aren't very reliable when it comes to fostering the better side of human nature. The goal is for the controls to be internal, and that just doesn't happen without giving kids practice at taking into account the concerns of other people. Yet the manner in which we often go about solving problems at school doesn't teach these skills at all! If you're using Plan A, then you're teaching the exact opposite: you're not being empathic, you're not taking into account the student's perspective, and you're not demonstrating an appreciation of how your behavior is affecting him.

We humans are vulnerable to being so convinced of the correctness of our position that we justify some of our worst behaviors with the belief that we're right. This is where we confuse the legitimacy of our *concerns* (which is a given) and the assumed justifiability of the *solutions* we're imposing, and lose track of our empathy and concern for others. If you're imposing solutions, it's guaranteed that someone else's concerns are being swept away. This is not what we want to be teaching students! And it's not how we want to go about solving problems with our students either.

The Invitation step also teaches students valuable skills, including considering the likely outcomes or consequences of one's actions; considering a range of solutions to a problem; shifting from one's original plan, idea, or solution; and taking into account situational factors that would suggest the need to adjust a plan of action.

How does the Invitation do that? Let's revisit what's going on in this step. You and the student are brainstorming solutions and evaluating the degree to which proposed solutions are realistic and mutually satisfactory. The realistic part gives you and the student invaluable practice at gauging whether both parties are capable of reliably executing their part of a solution. And the mutually satisfactory part gives you and the student practice at ensuring that the concerns of both parties are addressed.

Is it likely that the solution you envisioned prior to doing Plan B will be enacted? No, probably not. After all, you hadn't yet done the Empathy step when you envisioned that solution, and therefore the solution wasn't informed by the student's concerns. Is the solution the student envisioned prior to doing Plan B likely to be adopted? Probably not, since the solution he envisioned wasn't informed by *your* concerns. So you're both getting practice at moving off of your original solution.

The Invitation step will also help you and your students avoid the slippery slope toward power struggles. I'm often asked if I ever come across problems that simply cannot be solved in a mutually satisfactory manner. The answer is no. But what I do come across are lots of scenarios in which people have concluded that a problem is unsolvable because their competing solutions cannot be reconciled. That's because they've leapt right over concerns and jumped straight into solutions . . . *uninformed* solutions, which couldn't possibly take into account the concerns of both parties. As you know, there's no such thing as competing *concerns*. One party's concerns aren't more compelling or more important than the other's. Both parties' concerns need to be clarified and addressed. So the only reason a problem would be unsolvable is that there's no way to address the concerns of both parties. In my experience, that is a very rare occurrence.

Q & A

Question: What are the impacts of poverty and culture on the effectiveness of the CPS model?

Answer: The data suggest that socioeconomic status is not a predictor of success with the CPS model. Anecdotally, I've found that kids and adults from every culture and socioeconomic status want their concerns to be heard and addressed. And, in every culture, the probability of conflict is heightened when that doesn't occur.

Question: Can I use Plan B to involve my entire class in solving problems that affect all of them?

Answer: Absolutely. If there are unsolved problems that affect the entire class—often related to how kids are treating each other, but also related to things like hallway and cafeteria comportment—then it makes perfect sense to have the entire group voice concerns and work toward mutually satisfactory solutions.

Question: I'm beginning to recognize that we're not merely talking about how we should be solving problems with students; we're talking about how people should be solving problems with people. And I'm starting to think that my principal and superintendent need to learn more about Plan B.

Answer: Well, now, that wasn't a question; it was a statement.

EXPERIENCE IS THE BEST TEACHER

“The reason we're working with children is that we're passionate about them and we want to teach them. We don't only want to teach them academic skills. We want to teach them social skills too. A very important part of being human is learning those skills, like empathy. That's why we're here. We're here to help kids. And a teacher's time is very precious. You can feel the pressure of the mandates and everything like that. But we're taking the precious time that we spend with kids working on those skills. Kids are worth the investment of our time.”

—KATIE, LEARNING CENTER TEACHER

“I think it's important to remember that the social and emotional aspect goes hand in hand with academics. I think it's hard for teachers. We have all these things that we have to teach. We have to meet standards. But students are not going to be able to meet those standards if they don't deal with the social-emotional part first.

At the beginning of each school year, I let the entire class know that I'll be talking with them about different things that might come up. It's the same language no matter which kid it is and no matter what the problem. So the kids really get used to the idea, ‘Oh, I see her really being open to working with kids, and I know that it's OK if something happens in the classroom, that she's going to be there to help all of us.’ The kids start to see you as a partner.”

—KATHY, TEACHER

“I've had parents tell me, ‘Oh, I know that my child must be talking like you because they're saying, "I'm noticing" or "I'm wondering."’ It's so funny because the parents are saying, ‘They never talked like that before.’”

—KATIE, LEARNING CENTER TEACHER

“Kids now understand when another kid is having a hard time, and that it's OK. So if a child needs to leave the room or go for a walk, I used to think the other kids would say, ‘That's not fair. I want to go for a walk too.’ But that's not what they say. They say, ‘Oh, he's just having a hard time. He'll be back later. He's getting what he needs.’”

—KATIE, LEARNING CENTER TEACHER

"When I was a kid, I was well behaved at school. But I remember how painful it was to watch kids get in trouble year after year as a student. You'd be like, 'Please don't . . .' You almost want to wish them back into their seat or wish . . . 'Please do your paper. You're just going to get in so much trouble.' And then to have them get yelled at in front of everyone. So it's really nice now when kids see us solving problems with them, and not just with the difficult kids but all of them. We're who we want to be now. We're modeling who we want them to be and how we want them to treat each other."

—KATIE, LEARNING CENTER TEACHER

"It feels good to feel helpful. We're in a profession where we only have the kids for a little while. But we plant the seeds, and we hope they grow. And we see those buds coming out of the soil by the time they're leaving our school. It feels good. It brings morale for the whole school up. It makes coming to work feel fun and enjoyable and that you're really helping."

—BRIE, SCHOOL COUNSELOR

"I think we always loved our students and knew our students, but not at the level that we do now because of the problem solving. Now we're so much more invested, and we know them on such a deeper level through the conversations we've had with them. That gets passed on to the next year's teacher, who then is ready to jump in because he or she is hearing all of what we know and love about the kids and all of the positives and all of the great things about them."

—VICKI, DIRECTOR OF COMMUNICATIONS

"Whenever I hear about a kid being shackled or manhandled at school—as we've seen in the media recently—I say to myself, 'I wish that kid was at our school. I wish we had a chance with him.' Because I think we would have known that the student had a lot of lagging skills and unsolved problems and was having a hard time, whether it was behavioral or friendships. But we're solving problems with them so they have better ways to solve problems than violence. You find out what's behind it. Instead of just saying, 'You don't mean that; now I'm going to have to call your parents,' we say, 'What's going on that's making you feel that way?' And then you help them solve that problem. They don't feel like they have to hurt people or hurt a building or things like that anymore."

—KATIE, LEARNING CENTER TEACHER

❝❝That's why it's so important to build those relationships. There are a lot of kids who just need help solving the problems that affect their lives.❞❞

—VICKI, DIRECTOR OF COMMUNICATIONS

❝❝We had a year when we had a lot of pushback from parents of well-behaved kids. It was turning into a witch hunt. They wanted to see immediate consequences for misbehavior. They wanted to see that these kids were punished for what they were doing. Their own children were telling them that the behaviorally challenging kids weren't getting punished for what they were doing. But we called all the parents together, and there was a lot of anger about the kids who were acting up in school. Then I met with each parent individually. And I listened to them. A lot of what they were upset about was stuff that was in the grapevine and simply wasn't true. But when they heard what we were trying to do, and how we were trying to help the most vulnerable kids in our building, they completely chilled. We have nothing to hide in helping our tough kids. The year after that, those parents were integral to helping us create the learning center in our school, where kids and teachers go to get help solving problems together.❞❞

—NINA, PRINCIPAL

❝❝And I think we keep each other in check, as a staff, because if one of us starts to get really frustrated, someone else will say, 'Well, remember what we're about.' I think we do for each other.❞❞

—ANONYMOUS, EDUCATIONAL TECHNICIAN

❝❝I think parents can sometimes intimidate teachers. And I think sometimes teachers respond by defending themselves or justifying themselves. I think that's what can be hard.❞❞

—ALANNA, TEACHER

❝❝I think we take the judgment piece out with parents just as we did with the kids.❞❞

—NINA, PRINCIPAL

❝❝We used to say things like that a kid doesn't get any support from his parents with his homework. But what do we know about that family? We know nothing. We really don't know what happens at home. The kid still needs us to do our thing at school. If we know the kid is not going to get the homework support at home, we need to solve the problem with the kid so that the work can get done at school."

—ALANNA, TEACHER

"We're human. We're fallible. We can get threatened by maybe a parent or get nervous about it just because they're questioning what we're doing. But it's OK to acknowledge that we don't have all the answers. That's why we're collaborative."

—NINA, PRINCIPAL

"I've told parents that I've made mistakes with their child. Then we went back and figured out how to solve the problem. No one's judgmental. No one's overpowering anyone."

—ALANNA, TEACHER

"I actually had a parent tell me the other night, 'My son was struggling with something for the last four or five days. And he finally stopped and looked and he said, "Mom, you're supposed to be in the Empathy step. You're not supposed to tell me what to do right now. You're supposed to listen to me and show me that you care about what I have to say."'"

—TOM, ASSISTANT SUPERINTENDENT

"If we don't take the time to do Plan B, then we are sabotaging ourselves because of all the time it takes to repeatedly 'discipline' the same kids. So on a selfish, adult level, if we don't take time to do this, then we're spinning our wheels, doing the same ineffective things over and over again."

—CAROL, PRINCIPAL

"I think CPS has allowed us to be more compassionate. I've heard teachers from other schools talk about our school. They were saying things like, 'Oh, you let your kids do whatever they want.' And I got really defensive and said, 'That is such a misconception.' People can say what they want, and that's just noise. You have to remember that."

—ALANNA, TEACHER

❝I have a teacher who has embraced the model to the level where she does not just use CPS with highly challenging students; she uses it with all her students and builds it into her day. It is a reminder that often universal strategies for instruction, which benefit struggling learners, can be of benefit to all students. Whenever this teacher begins with 'I've noticed that . . .' to one particular student, he always smiles and says to her, 'It must be problem-solving time again!'❞

—RYAN, ASSISTANT PRINCIPAL

❝If you experience this and you get it, it gets in you and you want to do it more.❞

—TOM, ASSISTANT SUPERINTENDENT

Page references followed by fig indicate an illustration.